HISTORIC BALTIMORE

Twelve Walking Tours of Downtown, Fells Point, Locust Point, Federal Hill & Mount Clare

By Priscilla L. Miles

Library of Congress Catalog
Card Number: 86-091306

ISBN-0-9619542-3-X

CONTENTS

INTRODUCTION

I imagine that those of you who grew up in Baltimore in the '30s and '40s, as I did, became accustomed to hearing the city described by out-of-towners as "a big hick town." I was never sure what this meant so . . . since I had no come back . . . I would change the subject. But it always made me mad. This was my home and I loved it. What right had anyone to criticize it? Why did so many do it? And what did they mean?

I knew that Baltimore had made major contributions to the history of our country; the Star Spangled Banner, both the anthem and the flag, had come from here. The first railroad station in the world, the first steam engine, America's only umbrella factory, the Oriole baseball club, and the first Roman Catholic Bascilica to be built in the United States were all here.

And people such as Johns Hopkins, Moses Sheppard, Enoch Pratt, George Peabody, Henrietta Szold, H. L. Mencken, Babe Ruth and Russell Baker had worked here.

Pratt Library

Frederick Calvert, the sixth Lord of Baltimore.

Whatever did it take to be considered important? Money. And Baltimore was nicknamed Nickel City because more five cent pieces were spent here than anywhere else in the nation. Entertainment was cheap. Most Baltimoreans stayed home in the evening. If a couple did go out for dinner and to dance, they did not expect to pay much, nor did they dress up either. They took their evening clothes to night clubs in New York or San Francisco. Even Washington, D.C. And they spent their daytime hours taking tours in these cities, telling Baltimore friends about the sights they had seen, even showing pictures.

"There's a lot to see right here," I usually said.

"Other cities are much more interesting," was the answer.

"But this one is ours!" I must have raised my voice one time because a friend yelled back.

"Now listen, we are fed up with hearing you lecture about Baltimore. We don't want to hear it. You are *boring. Very boring* and it's time that somebody told you."

So I stopped.

Then on July 2, 1980, Harborplace opened. Two modest low-keyed buildings full of small specialty shops and gourmet restaurants had been built on cleared land in a harbor which H. L. Mencken had once described as smelling like a billion polecats. All kinds of Baltimoreans and people from out of town crowded into it.

They also saw new office buildings in the business district, rehabilitated early city houses in Otterbein, Federal Hill, and Fells Point, a World Trade Center designed by I. M. Pei, a Science Center, an Aquarium, and plans for thirteen new hotels in a city where four had once been more than adequate.

National magazines and newspapers began to print articles:

> Not so long ago "Bawlamer," as it's known locally, was thought of as a place to drive through on the way to someplace else.
>
> > The New York Times, Sunday August 14, 1983
> > Marion Burros. Travel Section

> In the years when this city was little more than a decaying traffic stop between New York and Washington the waiting room at the Mount Royal train station was equipped with rows of hard wooden rockers.
>
> In many ways the rockers symbolized what was then an insular, parochial city . . . Baltimore was Nickel City, a gustatory bargain basement, with a lazy Southern pace.

INTRODUCTION

*The rockers are long gone . . . and Baltimore is a
prime example of a Cinderella city. Once marked by
festering sores of urban decay, it has emerged as a
bustling, sophisticated metropolis.*
    The New York Times, Sunday, June 1, 1986
    Lindsey Gruson. Travel Section

There are reasons why Baltimore had developed
with such an insignificant image. Historically, the city
had been obliged to begin life in the shadows of its
more ostentatious sister ports: Boston, Philadelphia,
and Charleston. This happened quite simply because
these cities were older and had played more prominent roles in the establishment of Colonial America.[1]

In 1752, Baltimore was a small village of only 25
houses. By 1800 there were over three thousand
houses, the town had been incorporated as a city.
There was a Baltimore style clipper ship and the port
was beginning to receive international recognition for
its extensive wheat and tobacco exports, but it was
too late for the city to enjoy this new glory[2]. The damage to its self-image had been done. The inhabitants
had developed such a keen sense of inferiority that
they had assumed a rigid provincial attitude which
was to affect the city's business and social institutions
for two centuries. Even the invention of the railroad
which occurred in Baltimore in 1829 did nothing to
temper this feeling of inadequacy. Therefore, the Baltimore and Ohio railroad went bankrupt sixty-nine
years after its inception and was sold to out of state
entrepreneurs.[3]

Pratt Library

Early Baltimore, 1818.

INTRODUCTION

Fewer millionaires developed here than in Boston or New York. Fortunes were made in Baltimore, but the money was recycled within a small local circle in lieu of being invested more broadly.

Social problems such as public health and public safety were not readily heeded by the average citizen.

"The people of Baltimore, in their collective or municipal capacity, are the most silly, unreflective, procrastinating, impracticable and perverse congregation of bipeds to be found anywhere under the sun." Thus spoke Thomas Buckler, physician, in 1859.[4] He was expressing his frustrations which occurred while he and other concerned city officials attempted to design plans for waterworks and sewage control to halt the spread of contagious disease. People were dying of smallpox and cholera. Baltimoreans fussed and interfered with so many of the original plans for water-ways, drainage systems, and reservoirs that the city paid many times the amount it should have for the construction of these necessities.

And the loss of 1,545 buildings which occurred in the 1904 Baltimore fire would never have happened if city officials had been permitted to establish appropriate fire department regulations.

But that's the way it was. Today, the unique recreative work which the city has been forced to implement in the heart of its inner core in order to survive is bringing world-wide attention to Baltimore. Visitors and tourists are looking around and asking questions. Even the life-long residents are beginning to realize that their city is not as boring as they once thought it was. Maybe the provincial attitudes will dissipate as we answer, What is this city, Baltimore? Why did it develop?

The purpose of these walks is to help inquisitive people find their way in sections which answer these questions. The accompanying history is pertinent and anecdotal. Each walk is planned to last about an hour and a half — unless you stop to visit some of the sites. Enjoy.

NOTES Downtown Baltimore

▶ This land was once a part of John Eager Howard's estate and was known as Howard's woods. A portion of the French army camped here during the American Revolution. They drank water from a stream which ran where Center Street is now. It was a cold winter and their uniforms were torn and ragged. A group of Baltimore housewives, organized by Mrs. David Poe, made new uniforms for them. Mrs. Poe was the grandmother of Edgar Allan Poe. Mr. Poe was General Washington's quartermaster.

Pratt Library

The Basilica of the Assumption of the Blessed Virgin Mary.

▶ In 1789, The Reverend John Carroll was made the first bishop of the Roman Catholic Church in America. He was a brother of Charles Carroll of Carrollton, a patriot and a sophisticated person who was equipped to deal with an Anglican population.

He was "a man sent from God whose name was John," said the Cardinal.[1]

Father Carroll had been educated in France. He befriended Father Nagot of the French Sulpician Order at the time when that Order had been ousted from France. He invited them to Baltimore to found a seminary. Hence, St. Mary's Seminary came to be and the French Catholic tradition played a major role in Maryland Catholic education and administration.

1 This tour begins on Cathedral Street in front of
what is considered by many authorities to be the
most beautiful building in America. It is the Basilica
of the Assumption, designed by Benjamin H. Latrobe,
and constructed between 1808 and 1821. Latrobe also
designed the Capital of the United States, but the
Basilica is his masterpiece. He is the architect who
introduced the neo-classical or Greek Revival style
into American architecture. Some people felt the exterior of this building was more suggestive of a pagan
temple than a Christian Church. Note its warm, quiet
dignity. We're not sure how the minarets got placed
at the top. Latrobe's original drawings show two
rounded domes.

Once inside there is an immediate sense of spiritual
awe. Sit for a moment in one of the pews and absorb
the beauty. The plan is a Latin Cross. Part of the
explanation for its perfection lies with the way part
leads to part, the little to the big.[2] The rest is in the
intangible appeal to the senses.

The altar is a gift from France. So are the wonderful
bells in the domes. There is a portrait of Archbishop
Carroll on the south wall and there are other treasures
to be seen.

Tours may be arranged by calling 727-6534.

► Oddly, Enoch Pratt was not a reader, but he came from New England and a culture where books were revered. In Baltimore he manufactured nails, horse shoes, and shoes for mules. It is said he squeezed a penny until it squeaked, and if he saw a nail lying in the street, he would stop his carriage to retrieve it, because it could be used again. He belonged to a group of wealthy men who were competing with one another in endowing the city with noteworthy (and name preserving) institutions. Pratt gave $225,000 for a public library, plus an additional $33,333 if the city would promise to provide $50,000 for maintenance. It did. This was one of the pioneer public libraries in America. Pratt lived several blocks from here in a house which is now occupied by the Maryland Historical Society. The first library building was in this area and he hovered over every purchase until his death.[3]

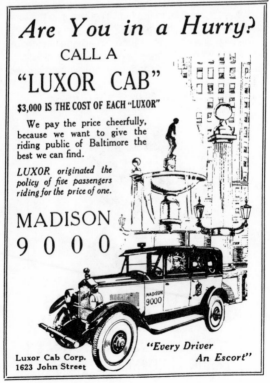

2 Across the street is the Central Branch of the Enoch Pratt Library, designed by Clyde N. Fritz with Tilden and Githens, and opened in 1933. It replaced the original Central Branch which opened in 1886. This building is many times larger, with a special room for Poe and for Mencken, a Maryland department, a separate section for children, a lovely new gift shop, and an extensive collection of history books, novels, sociology and psychology books, and an excellent reference desk where any question can be answered. Do go in. Browse or just look at the handsome lobby.

Open 10am — 9pm Monday-Thursday
10am — 5pm Friday & Saturday

The original Enoch Pratt Free Library.

3 Let's walk east on Mulberry Street, to Charles. The Latrobe house was in this block, John H. B. Latrobe, son of B. H. Latrobe lived in it for many years. He was the inventor of the Latrobe stove and he supplied the cigars and wine to a special literary committee while it read "The Ms Found in a Bottle." The story won a prize and was published in a local paper. Its author was an unknown Baltimorean named Edgar Allan Poe. It was this story that began Poe's career.

Baltimore Sun

Looking north on Charles Street, 1937.

▶ *The Woman's Exchange was started just after the Civil War in the front parlor of Mrs. H. Harmon Brown. Those were the days when the only money making projects for ladies of gentility were cooking and fine needlework. The War between the States had created economic problems and these particular ladies were forced to sell family heirlooms and do creative needlework in order to survive.*

This building was purchased in 1882 so their needlework could be displayed and sold. Notice the old tin lined ceilings and the original cashier's cage in the front of the store. You can still buy handmade quilts, knitted sweaters, fancy pillows and smocked dresses for little girls. And look for the men's work! The Woman's Exchange became coed in the 1970's.

4 The Archbishop's residence is on the northwest corner of Charles and Mulberry. It was designed by William Small and built in 1829. The hyphens and the third floor were added in 1865. In the 1950's the original stucco was covered with a sophisticated rendition of formstone. The house is late Federal style. It's an old Baltimore tradition to watch the garden for crocuses. Winters, in the past, have been quite severe. The sight of green tips bring a sense of relief and some praise for the Lord. "It won't be long now," Baltimoreans say.

5 405 N. Charles is Bowen and King. It's an optical firm which moved into this building from Liberty Street in 1914. It's the last of the veteran Charles Street stores in this block.

BOWEN & KING

Prescription Opticians

117 N. Liberty St.   Baltimore, Md.

---

6 One block south of here, at the corner of Charles and Pleasant Streets is another old Charles Street favorite: The Woman's Industrial Exchange, Inc. If you haven't had lunch, go have a bite and order chocolate charlotte russe for dessert. Everything is "made from scratch." Bread, cookies, cakes, preserves can be purchased from the shop in front of the dining room. Get some Maryland beaten biscuits. They are one of a kind.
Open Monday-Saturday, 11 am-2 pm.

Blanche Darnall Smith,   Rose Mae McCormick

MAISON AU CHOCOLAT
413 N. CHARLES STREET
BALTIMORE, MD.
BREAKFASTS, LUNCHES, AFTERNOON TEAS
SPECIAL ATTENTION TO TEAS, PARTIES, ETC.

▶ The Charles Street Association was formed in 1915 and is the oldest merchant's association in Maryland. It was a strict group with rigid requirements especially in relation to the appearance of store fronts. Its purpose was to preserve the character of Charles Street and they were never shy about blackballing a usurper. They had to struggle during the late 1950's and early '60's because many of the original stores: Kirk's Silver, Schoen Russell Hats, Hanna's Linens, Maison Annette and Schofield's closed or moved away. The C&P phone company owned this property and they took advantage of their opponents.

After the big fire in 1904, many of the small prestigious businesses moved into this area of Charles Street. There had been lovely homes in most of these buildings but the street car had been invented and the populace was moving northward. Owners were willing to sell to those businessmen and merchants who would maintain the quality and dignity which had been established in this district.

Mr. Brown completely reorganized the buildings which he bought, adding an arcade, storefronts, bay windows, and skylights. He expanded the arcade to include a building behind it which faced onto Saratoga Street. This created a short cut which became a favorite way for shoppers to reach the Howard Street Department Stores.

7 As you leave the Exchange glance at the large building on the opposite side of Pleasant Street. This is the C&P Telephone Company and it should not be here because it is too large and has spoiled the scale which was set for buildings on Charles Street in 1915. C&P sneaked their building in at a time when morale of Charles Street Merchants was very, very low. Some lovely old homes along Pleasant Street were destroyed to make room for this anachronism.

9 NORTH LIBERTY STREET
BALTIMORE

For over three score years the Stieff piano has occupied the highest position among the music-cultured people of America.

8 Brown's Arcade at 322-328 N. Charles Street was renovated by Struever Brothers and Eccles, Inc. and the Enterprise Development Co. in the late 1970's. In keeping with their philosophy to preserve the past, the developers have restored the vacant buildings to their previous character. The original had been planned in 1906 by former Maryland Governor, Frank Brown. The local firm of architects: Cho, Wilkes, and Benn did an outstanding job in assisting the Struevers to modernize the interiors of the shops. Wander around and look.

C. J. BENSON & COMPANY
INTERIOR DECORATIONS
325 NORTH CHARLES STREET

▶ *Unitarianism was a fledgling movement which was just beginning to emerge in New England in the early 19th Century. Its leaders had a hard time trying to organize a congregation in Baltimore, but they persisted. The theology of this group had attracted such independent thinkers as Thomas Jefferson, John Adams, his son Quincy, Louisa May Alcott, Ralph Waldo Emerson, and Susan B. Anthony. When these church doors opened in Baltimore, in October, 1818, it became the first Unitarian Church in the United States to be built for and by Unitarians.*

9 Now we'll walk north to Charles and Franklin Streets. On the northwest corner is the First Unitarian Church designed by Maximilian Godefroy in 1818. Note the simplicity of the structure—a cube surmounted by a hemisphere. This exterior is an excellent example of Roman Classicism. The terra-cotta sculpture (replaced in 1954 by Henry Berge) represents the Angel of Truth. The dome is modeled from the Pantheon in Rome.[4] When this church was built, all churches were rivalling one another in the attempt to "look different" from the rows of houses which surrounded them. They wanted to add a sense of culture to their environs. Domes were the "in thing." This is the third one in a four block radius.

Notice the large placard on the right side front of the building. The Unitarians call this their "Wayside Pulpit." The message is printed in large print to be readily legible to drivers and walkers in this area. Many of us ponder it as we go northward.

Unhappily, a fire in the late '60's destroyed a portion of the interior including the organ which Godefroy had designed. The interior is interesting. The original pulpit is there, the baptismal font and the design under the dome. Admission may be gained by phoning: 685-2330.

10 As we walk on northward, we pass Tomlinson's Craft Store and Louie's Book Store. Both are recent newcomers to Charles Street but each is interesting so stop in and browse. There is a nice little cafe in the bookstore if you're in need of something to eat or drink.

11 As we cross Center Street and start up the hill we enter Mount Vernon Square which many still think is the heart of Baltimore. It really is the most gracious, the most elegant, and the least changed of any early 19th section of Baltimore.

You might prefer to walk along the path in the center of the park. It is one of four which surround the Washington Monument. This particular portion contains a charming little statue, "The Sea Urchin" by Henry Berge, Sr., and an equestrian statue of the Marquis de Lafayette by Andrew O'Connor.

▶ In Europe, by 1800, the large excavations of ancient Greece had begun. Pompeii and Herculaneum had been uncovered. Ancient Greece architecture began to be copied to such an extent that from 1820-1855 it became a mania.

In America, Thomas Jefferson wanted to create a national style based on the archeology of the Roman Empire, but no one paid attention to him. Instead, European trained persons such as B.H. Latrobe and Maximilian Godefroy brought Greece to Baltimore. This is why we have such fancy words as "neoclassism" and "Greek revival" used in the descriptions of so many of our buildings. It is also why the wealthy could have Ionic, Doric or Corinthian columns beside their front door. Mount Vernon Square is an excellent reflection of this time.

▶ Henry Walters came to Baltimore from Philadelphia about 1841, just after the Susquehanna River Canal was opened. He became a controlling director in the Baltimore and Susquehanna Railroad. He had a commission business dealing in the beginning with shipping produce only to Pennsylvania. In 1847 he added liquor, both foreign and domestic, to his inventory of goods. Then he became aware of the need for fast freight to ship perishable produce from the South to the North. He consolidated some bankrupt railroad lines to meet this purpose and made himself vulnerable to capture because of his southern sympathies in the War Between the States. He left America to spend four years in Paris. It was there that he began to amass the amazing collection of paintings, sculptures, and Eastern ceramics which comprise a portion of the Walters collection. When he returned to Baltimore, he lived at 8 Mount Vernon Place and opened the house several times a week to anyone who wished to see his art. Henry, his son, shared his father's love of art as well as his father's genius for making money. He enlarged the collection and built the museum to house it. When Henry died in 1931, he left the collection to the City of Baltimore together with $2,000,000 to be used in its maintenance.[5]

12 The Walters Art Gallery, designed by William A. Delano, and built between 1905-1910 is on your left. The plan for the building is based on the University of Genoa's University Palace. It's not a very inspiring facade, but peek inside! It's so simple and so magnificent and so intimate that you may never leave.

It houses one of the largest private collections in the country and certainly the most diversified. Scholars are intrigued with the broad range of the Walters' interests. The Byzantine silver collection is the finest in the world. There is a fantastic variety of ivories from the Medieval period, and the art collection is all-encompassing beginning with the Ancient Period and extending through the ages to the end of the 19th century.

The Gallery is open Tuesday-Sunday: from 11 am-4:30 p.m. Admission fee. Tours are given daily. Phone: 547-5000.

PERSONALS

13 Pause at the corner of Charles Street and Monument to look at the quietly elegant houses which face onto the square. These were the homes of the wealthy from the early 1840's until they moved to the northern sections in the 1920's. Each house had a carriage house behind it and you can see these if you poke around a bit. Each house had accommodations for live-in servants. Extraneous help—such as laundresses—lived in nearby alley houses. The appearance of the Square has barely changed in 100 years. The houses now are apartments, condominiums, or doctors offices. Two of them contain prestigious clubs. Others house Peabody Institute students.

The Park was laid out in 1832 by Thomas Poppleton and was the first Park in the city. It was landscaped by Frederick Olmsted, Senior. It's purpose was to increase the value of the adjacent land. It is an example of a Baroque city square and is probably the best such design in the nation. The walkways, fountains and statues were added in the early 1900's.[6]

▶ All of this land belonged originally to John Eager Howard, a Revolutionary hero and benefactor to Baltimore. His estate was named "Belvidere" and the house was located where the Belvedere hotel is today. His statue is in the north square. The facades of these homes are not nearly as ostentatious as their counterparts in Newport and New York although their owners were equally as wealthy. These doorways bespeak the conservatism, the reserve, and the pride — false or otherwise — which is the core of the Baltimore character.

▶ Barye's chief interest was in sculpting animals. William Walters was among the first to realize the man's talents and he brought a superior collection of Baryes from France to Baltimore, The artist never received recognition until he was quite elderly.

"Finally," he is rumored to have remarked, "they bring me things to eat when I no longer have any teeth."[7]

▶ The houses here are identified by the names of original owners as well as by number. There's no special reason for this — just habit.

▶ Baltimoreans waged one of their internal battles with the city while they waited for the statue of Lafayette. The original plan had been to place it at the eastern end of Mount Vernon Place. A ceremony was held and the ground was broken in 1918. In 1919 a marble base for the statue appeared on the southern side of the square near the foot of the Washington Monument. In 1920 or so the Sunpapers printed a picture of the base with the caption: "Here we are, Lafayette, where the hell are you?" In 1924, the statue was finally mounted and the people complained that the General looked malnourished.[8] See what you think.

14 The large bronze lion in the square in front of you is by Antoine Louis Barye and is an exact copy of one in the Tuileries in Paris. The four bronze groupings on the cement cornerstones are also copies by Barye of originals which are in the Louvre. They are titled: War, Peace, Force, and Order. Barye was the leading sculptor of his time. His work was a gift to the city from the Walters.

15 1 West Mt. Vernon Place is the Thomas-Jencks-Gladding House designed by J. R. Niernsee and J. C. Nielson, architects, and built 1849-1851. It is an Italianate-style house which was originally painted. Note the heavy cornice, the protruding corners, and the casements. These illustrate a trend in building which became quite popular in mid-nineteenth century American. The house has recently become a part of the Walters Complex and will contain its collection of Asian Art.

Pratt Library

Mt. Vernon Place West, about 1910, showing the Barye bronzes.

▶ The Garretts had made their fortune with the development of the Baltimore and Ohio Railroad, but they had not "made it" into the social spheres until Robert Garrett married Mary Frick. He did not live very long after the marriage and she then married Dr. Henry Barton Jacobs. Mary Garrett, sister to Robert lived just around the corner on Cathedral Street. It was she, together with her friends, who made the Hopkins medical school available to women.

▶ A man named Henry Pratt Janes lived at 13 Mount Vernon Place and he objected so strongly to the addition put on the Jacobs house by Stanford White that he took the case to court and won. The vestibule, he said, interrupted his light, his air, and his view of the Washington Monument. Mrs. Jacobs somehow managed to have the court reverse its opinion. She was not going to have a "nobody" cause her to change her plans. Then, in 1915, she bought #13 and demolished the entire back of it so that she might have light and air. Actually, she was having her revenge on Mr. Janes.

▶ Francis Scott Key died in the house which was on the spot where the church is today. Roger Brooke Taney, whose statue is in the west square, was his brother-in-law. Taney became attorney general under Andrew Jackson and later Chief Justice of the Supreme Court.

16 7 to 11 Mount Vernon Place is the Engineering Society, designed by Sanford White and John Russell Pope, and built 1884-1902. It is three houses, made into one. It was once the Garrett-Jacobs house and is considered to be the largest, the most imposing, and the costliest town house ever built in Baltimore. It was the creation of Mary Frick Garrett, first the wife of Robert Garrett, Jr. and then the wife of Henry Barton Jacobs. She was the grand dame of her day and she was one who did not adhere for one moment to the provincial tone of the town. She was as formidable and as all-controlling of the social world in Baltimore as her counterpart in New York, Mrs. John Jacob Astor. Numbers 9 and 11 were turned into one house by Stanford White about 1894. Number 7 was added in 1902 by John Russell Pope because Stanford White had managed to anger Mrs. Jacobs. The carved wooden spiral stairway is thought to be designed by White, and so are the Tiffany glass windows. Once completed the house contained 40 rooms and a roofed conservatory which held doves, palm trees and a running stream. The outside was faced with brownstone.[9]

17 Note the "Boy with Turtle" by Creier in the fountain.

18 Let's cross to the north side. Number 8 West Mount Vernon Place is the Mount Vernon Club. Known as the Tiffany-Fisher House it was built about 1842 and is one of the finest Greek Revival Town Houses in Baltimore. It has a simple painted brick facade with a Doric columned Portico. It has been a private woman's club since 1942.

19 Washington Place is the name for the northern wing of Mount Vernon Place and at 700 is the Washington Apartments, designed by Edward Glidden, built in 1906, at the time when apartment living was only for the rich. It is now a condominium. This is an elaborate building in the Beaux Arts style. The walls and ceiling of the foyer and lobby have recently been refurbished with gold leaf. Have a look.

▶ *The rectory is named for Francis Asbury, first Bishop of the Methodist Church in America.*

▶ *The Mount Vernon Place Methodist Church was the most elegant of all the churches in Baltimore. It cost $320,000 to build, had the largest organ in the city and held a "brilliantly lit up" nighttime auction for the choice of pews.[10]*

▶ *These brownstone houses were a real estate adventure financed by Richard France, known as the lottery king, in Baltimore. They were an immediate success.*

Prait Library

Brownstone houses on East Mt. Vernon Place.

▶ *George Peabody was one of the richest men in the world. He was born in Danvers, Massachusetts in 1795. His family was poor so at eleven years of age the boy left school and went to work as an apprentice in a grocery store in Salem. Five years later he was given a suit of "good clothes," thirty dollars in silver and sent to Washington to live with an uncle who was a merchant. He enlisted in the War of 1812 and, at Fort McHenry, he met a Baltimorean named Elisha Riggs. When the war ended the two set up a dry goods business and named it: Riggs, Peabody and Company. Peabody was just twenty years old, but he had an instinctive understanding of financial matters which helped the business to grow and to expand to other cities.*

20 The Mount Vernon Place Methodist Church, designed by Thomas Dixon and Charles L. Carson and built in 1870-1872. It's a wonderfully elegant and graceful building, made of a green marble named serpentine. This substance does not weather well and the church was completely repaired in 1932 and 1978. It's a pretty church with some nice rose windows. Phone: 685-5290 for admission.

21 10 East Mount Vernon Place is Asbury House, designed by J. R. Niernsee and J. C. Neilson, and built about 1855. It currently contains the rectory and business office of the Mount Vernon Place Methodist Church.

22 22 to 32 East Mount Vernon Place is known as brownstone row. They illustrate the brownstone facades which became popular in most American cities during the 1860's.

23 The Peabody Institute and Library are on the southeast corner of East Mount Vernon Place. It was built between 1857 and 1878, at a time when Baltimore had no library, no art gallery, no academy of music, and no auditorium of any sort for scholarly lectures. The Peabody provided for all of these. The rather formal Renaissance Revival facade belies the wonderful inside. The west wing contains the concert hall (which was rehabilitated in 1982-1983), music rooms and classrooms.

The east wing contains the library. This is a magnificent room, six open floors high, supported with cast-iron columns and railings, supplied with 250,000 rare and valuable books, and furnished with a beautiful Beaver Dam marble floor. John Dos Passos loved this

George Peabody Statue.

▶ When Peabody was forty-two he moved to England where he made an incredible fortune selling U.S. bond issues in Europe during the American Civil War.[11] He never came back to Baltimore, but he never forgot his plan to do something worthwile for the city. He was quite specific.

He wanted his conservatory to be a place of learning not only for students, but for everyone in Baltimore. Peabody was also generous with his money in England. Queen Victoria offered him a baroncy which he refused because it would have cost him his American citizenship.

room and did most of his research here. The library is a work of art, yet few Baltimoreans know that it exists.... Despite its rich heritage, the Peabody has had financial problems. In 1982, the library became a department of the Johns Hopkins University.

The library is open Monday-Saturday from 9 am to 5 pm. Don't miss looking at it!

Pratt Library

The Peabody Library.

Pratt Library

The country setting of the Washington Monument, 1829.

▶ *The original intention of the city was to place the monument in the center of town where the Battle Monument is today, but there were town houses on both sides of the street. Citizens were afraid the column would tumble over and crumble the houses or kill the people walking on the street. So John Eager Howard donated a vacant field which sat on his property at the crest of a hill, a mile away from the center of town yet close enough for the monument to be visible. John Ridgely of Hampton, in Baltimore County, donated the marble. The fence around the base was donated by Robert Carey Long, Jr. It was quite similar to the iron fence which surrounded all of Mount Vernon Place when it was first developed.*

▶ *The presence of the monument was and is a quietly eloquent testimony to the loyalty the State and the citizens of Baltimore have felt for their country and its father.*

24 The Washington Monument is the beautiful column of marble in the center of Mount Vernon Place. It was completed in 1829 five years before the one in Washington, D.C. was begun. It has just been thoroughly cleaned and restored.

The column is 160 feet high. The statue of Washington, sculpted by Italian Enrico Causici, stands 16 feet.

It depicts the general resigning his commission as Commander of the Continental Army. A contest was held in 1815 to select an architect. It was won by Robert Mills, a student of B. H. Latrobe. Then a lottery was created in order to raise the more than $100,000 it cost to build the shaft.

The construction was a considerable architectural achievement for its time and remains so. Let's stroll over and enter the room at its base. There is a modest fee and the climb to the top is 228 steps. Once there you have the city of Baltimore at your feet. What better place is there for us to leave you?

Pratt Library

Charles Street looking north to the Monument.

1. *Morris Mechanic Theatre*
2. *B&O Building*
3. *Old Savings Bank of Baltimore*
4. *Former North German Lloyd Steamship Co.*
5. *Sun Life Building*
6. *Blaustein Building*
7. *Charles Center South*
8. *Garmatz Federal Office Building*
9. *Civic Center—Baltimore Arena*
10. *Mercantile Safe Deposit and Trust Building*
11. *Omni International Hotel*
12. *Hamburger's Store*
13. *One Charles Center*
14. *Old Central Savings Bank*
15. *Fidelity Building*
16. *Masonic Temple*
17. *Old St. Paul's Protestant Episcopal Church*
18. *Commercial Credit Annex*
19. *First YMCA*
20. *Old St. Paul's Rectory*
21. *St. Alphonsus Church*
22. *Marconi's Restaurant*

NOTES Downtown Baltimore

▶ *Charles Street has long been considered Balti-more's most important north-south roadway. In the 1920's-1940's this particular section contained the most exclusive shops in town. Then the move to the suburbs began in earnest.*

In 1952, a report from the Commission on Govern-mental Economy and Efficiency summarized the financial status of Baltimore City with this bleak state-ment: "Unless radical action is taken, the municipal corporation will be bankrupt within a generation." Urban deterioration was killing the city's commerce, industry, transportation, cultural life, housing develop-ment, and community well being. The reality of the situation shook the business community into action. They moved quickly.

In 1953, the Committee for Downtown was formed.

In 1954, the Greater Baltimore Committee devel-oped. Together, these two groups raised enough money to hire a city planner. The most astute men in the city were asked to offer their business and finan-cial expertise to implement city projects.

In March, 1958, a plan for Charles Center was pre-sented to the Mayor. 33 acres of downtown property were to be revamped, Outmoded office buildings were to be replaced with new ones. Landscaped malls and walkways were to replace some streets. Off-street parking was to be put underground.

In November, 1958, voters approved a $35,000,000 urban renewal loan to activate the construction.

In 1962, the first new building, One Charles Center, was completed. The implementation of the Charles Center plan paved the way for the inner harbor development ten years later. The miracle which was created is now history.

1 Let's begin this tour at the intersection of Charles and Baltimore Streets. This is the symbolic double axis of Baltimore. It is the point where the city literally divides: north, south, east, and west. It's not a pretty corner, but it is an important one. It was once known as Sun Square because the Sunpaper Building was here for over fifty years and people used to gather to get the news first hand. The paper moved in 1949 and its place has been taken by the Mechanic Theater. Walk west on Baltimore Street to a point where you can see the theater in toto. It was designed by John Johanson in 1967. He described it as "functional expressionism." The outside form is intended to reflect the spaces or activities of the interior.[1] It's one of the most dramatic of the group of structures which comprise Charles Center.

Pratt Library

The Old Baltimore Sun Building.

▶ In the plan for "The Temple of Thrift" employers were persuaded to open accounts on behalf of their employees. Prudent investment and honest savings were to earn interest for old age and ill health. There were no stockholders to share profits so interest and profit could be divided among the depositors. The first day's take was $170.00, deposited by nine persons — a caterer, a tavern keeper, two tailors, a barber, a clerk, a baker, a schoolmaster, and a housewife.[3]

Unhappily, the grandeur of the bank's interior was spoiled by changes made in 1953.

B&O Archives

Doorway of the B&O Building.

2 Now let's return to Charles Street. On the northwest corner is the magnificent building designed by Parker and Thomas in 1906 to house the offices for the Baltimore and Ohio Railroad. The first building was destroyed in the Baltimore fire. This one was constructed immediately there- after. It has recently been renovated and you must go in to see the magnificent lobby. Jacques Kelly has said, "At least half of Northern Italy seems to be represented in marble."[2]

3 On the southeast corner is the Savings Bank of Baltimore — once known as "The Temple of Thrift." It was formed in 1818 by a group of Quakers which included Elisha Tyson and Moses Sheppard. Its purpose was to encourage "the industrious poor to save." It's interesting to note that when 15 Baltimore banks either closed or operated on a limited withdrawal basis in the depression years (1931-1934) The Savings Bank of Baltimore met all of its depositors' demands without having to borrow a penny.

The bank moved into this building in 1907. It was designed by Parker, Thomas and Rice and was inspired by the Erechtheum which stands on the Acropolis in Athens. The lion heads that decorate the cornice were copied from casts which actually came from Athens. The building is constructed from Beaver Dam marble and is an excellent example of neo-classical revival style architecture which was popular in Baltimore at the turn of the century.[4]

4 Let's stroll south on Charles Street. Note the unique building on the northeast corner of Charles at Redwood. It was built in 1907 for the North German Lloyd Steamship Company. Designed by Parker, Thomas and Rice, its model was a German building in the 1900 Paris Exposition.

▶ The Sun Life is the first office building on our tour which illustrates the Charles Center complex. In its lobby is an interesting piece of sculpture by Dimitri Hadzi that hangs from the ceiling.

▶ In 1917, as more and more people were driving their new cars into town, a man named Jacob Blaustein began to deliver kerosene in a horse-drawn tank car down Baltimore Street so drivers could have fuel for the return home. In 1923, he built the first drive-in filling station, named The Lord Baltimore, on Cathedral Street. Fuel sellers were not always honest. Blaustein put a ten gallon graduated jar on top of his pumps together with a sign which read, "You see what you get. You get what you see." This gasoline was sold under the American Oil Label. By 1928, he had obtained control of Crown Central Petroleum and moved its offices into Baltimore. Blaustein's commercial theory was to make the public "brand conscious" and he used color to do this. Thus evolved the Crown Stations with blue and red/orange colors. The company's concept of a multipump station with twenty-four hour service has proven to be a trendsetter in the business.[5]

Pratt Library

Policeman at the corner of Charles and Saratoga Streets.

5 On your right is the Sun Life Building, designed in 1966 by Peterson, Brickhauer and Emory Roth and Sons. It is faced with nonreflective black Canadian granite and has a separate steel super-structure which rests on four large steel columns anchored in bedrock.

6 1 N. Charles Street is the Blaustein Building, designed by Vincent Kling, completed in 1963. Gossip says the Blausteins wanted their building to be where One Charles Center is located. When they did not get that spot they built this building in such a way that a large portion of the view of Baltimore is blocked from One Charles Center.

7 Charles Center South is the name of the building on the south corner of Charles and Lombard Streets. It's an unusual hexagonal shape, designed by RTKL Associates, Inc. and completed in 1975. The architects had planned a taller building which would have made a more elegant corner, but we think the dark gray glass panels are stunning and are a good contrast to its neighbors.

8 Let's turn right and walk over Lombard Street to Hopkins Place. On your left is the Edward A. Garmatz Federal Office Building, designed by RTKL Associates, Inc. and finished in 1976. The building has been described as looking like "an IBM card with all the holes punched."[6] The sculpture in front is by George Sugarman and helps to distract a bit from the severe look of the entrance.

9 We'll turn right onto Hopkins Place. The Civic Center on your left was built in 1968 in order to add importance to the Charles Center Plan. Many persons felt that this arena should have been built in the suburbs. The first City Fair was held here in 1969 and the Civic Center has been the focus for many sports events, the Barnum and Bailey Circus, rock concerts, and all sorts of activities which are conducive to life in the city. We think the spot has been appropriate.

▶ *The Baltimore Office of Promotion and Tourism opened its first office here in 1969. Tourism has grown to be the second most lucrative business in Baltimore. The new office is located in The Brokerage — several blocks east of here.*

▶ *Isaac Hamburger came to Baltimore from Neidenburg, Germany in 1845. He started to work as a cutter in a clothing store. Ten years later he began his own wholesale trade which he combined with a retail one in a plant on Pratt Street. Soon he had 13 stores and a distribution center.*

10 The new Mercantile Safe Deposit and Trust Company Building is on the southeast corner of Hopkins Place and Baltimore Street. It was designed by Peterson, Brickhauer, Emory Roth and Sons and completed in 1969. The lobby is rather austere, but the building contains the offices of several major law offices and accounting firms.

11 The Omni International Hotel is a subdued two towered building. It is low keyed and functions as a comfortable anchor for its place in Charles Center. Let's turn right at Fayette Street and return to Charles.

12 Hamburger's Store, on the southeast corner. The building adds an esthetic grace to this portion of Charles Center and it is the city's oldest retail clothing firm. There has been a Hamburger's store in Baltimore since 1855. The extension over Fayette Street is a portion of the Charles Center walkway.

Pratt Library

Charles Street north from Saratoga.

NOTES Downtown Baltimore

▶ *The career of Mies van der Rohe began in Germany in the 1920's when the German Stuttgart government assigned him to design a worker-housing exhibit. He abolished every bit of ornamentation which could possibly be considered bourgeois and developed a formula for flat roofs, no cornices, sheer walls, no window decorations, no pediments, no color. It demonstrated the simple use of inexpensive industrial materials. The people loved it . . . In 1937, because of his anti-Hitler sentiments, van der Rohe came penniless to the United States where he began to be paid fantastic sums to utilize his formula for apartment houses and office buildings. Tom Wolfe has said: "van der Rohe has put half of America inside German workers' housing cubes, made to serve every purpose except housing for workers."*[7]

T. Chandlee

One Charles Center by Mies van der Rohe.

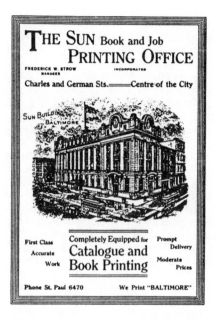

13 Let's turn left and look at One Charles Center. It is the masterpiece of the Complex, designed by Ludwig Mies van der Rohe, completed in 1962. The building is somber, and it is elegant. It is here because J. Jefferson Miller, the President of the Committee for Downtown Baltimore told van der Rohe that if he would enter the design competition which was being held for buildings to be erected in Charles Center he would win. (So it's said, by those in the know at the time.) The building took 13 months to complete and cost about $10,350,000. Very reasonable for a van der Rohe. It is similar to his epoch-making Seagram Building in New York City. Go inside and look. The plaza is paved with travertine. The lobby walls are lined with green Tines marble.

14 Across the street is the old Central Savings Bank building designed by George Frederick in 1890, now used as an outlet for Radio Shack. It was Baltimore's first combination bank and commercial building. There is still some wonderful woodwork along sections of the fifth floor.

▶ Prior to World War II this section of Charles Street was the center of specialty shopping for the elite. The only survivor of that era is Downs Stationery Store at 317 N. Charles Street.

Downs was once important because it contained the debutante list for the year and a social calendar for all important dates such as weddings and debutante parties. Often families scheduled a special date two years before a party for their debutante was given. The store also had the appropriate paper or card for the invitation. Dies made for calling cards or initialed writing paper could be and still are kept on file. The Blue Book known as the Baltimore Society Visiting List (founded in 1888) is still published by Downs. It has always been described as "a register of the Society of Baltimore with members residing in Maryland and out-of-state, the debutante list and calendar, maiden names of brides, and officers of leading clubs." The cost of the book has escalated with the years from $5.00 to $45.00. Not many old Baltimore families are still listed. Their names can be found in the Social Register which is printed in New York.

Baltimore Sun

Old St. Paul's Church, 1931.

▶ The spiritual component of the Church of England, from which the Episcopal Church descends, was at a low ebb in America in the early days. In 1739, George Whitefield considered Maryland among "the dark corners of the earth . . . a place as yet unwatered with the true Gospel of Christ."

15 The Fidelity Building, on the northwest corner, was designed by Baldwin and Pennington and built in 1893. The first eight floors are solid granite. The upper stories were added in 1912-1915 and are faced with terra cotta. The Central Savings Bank and the Fidelity Building are two downtown buildings which were saved from demolition when the Charles Center Plan was implemented.

16 223-225 N. Charles Street was built in 1869 to be a Masonic Temple. Joseph E. Sperry, architect, added the present roof in 1909 after the first was destroyed by a fire. It is thought that the entrance is probably his, also.

17 Old St. Paul's Protestant Episcopal Church, Mother Church in Baltimore, has a history almost a century older than that of the first Episcopal Diocese in America. The Parish was established in 1692. The first church was built in what is now Fort Holabird in East Baltimore. That church burned, and in 1730 plans were made to build the second church on this site because it was the highest point of land in Baltimore Town and was, therefore, several steps closer to Heaven.[9] That church was finished in 1739. There were more fires. Robert Cary Long, Sr. built a third church on this site in 1814. That too burned. This present building was erected on the foundations of the Long one in 1856 by Richard Upjohn, an architect whose specialty was churches. He had rebuilt Trinity Church in New York City in 1839. The style of this building is Italian Romanesque basilica with a high tower (never completed) on the northwest corner. The two loggia with bas relief panels were carved by Antonio Capellane for the 1814 church. The windows are by Louis Comfort Tiffany.[10] Phone: 685-3404 to gain entrance.

If you glance down Saratoga Street toward the east, you can gain an impression of the steepness of the Jones Falls Valley. The land has been filled in, plowed down and made liveable. It was not pretty when Baltimore was young. There were marshes, buffs and crags of red clay. It's still not the handsomest of views.

Parsons were more interested in fox hunting than in saving souls. After the Revolution, the Episcopal Church lost most of its clergy as well as the tobacco tax which had supported it.[8] Happily St. Paul's Parish survived. Some thirty years ago the vestry put up the large glass doors which have enabled passers-by to enjoy the softly lit altar at night. It is a reassuring sight and a comforting one.

The cross from the third church was removed from the ruins of the third fire and placed on the roof of Church Hospital. It's still there.

▶ Commercial Credit Company developed with the auto age. Its founders were the innovators for financing new automobiles on the installment plan. The company was also responsible for beginning a national trend. In the early 1920's so many automobiles were being driven into town that some way had to be developed to park them. The idea of "stacking" them into a four level garage with ramps was discussed. The Commercial Credit Building is built on the foundations of the St. Paul Street garage, the first in the city to offer such an "unusual" parking arrangement.

St. Paul's Rectory, 1928.

▶ Many famous and interesting people have visited the Rectory through the years. Carl Sandburg was one. He is said to have compared the winding staircase to a staff of musical notes. All of St. Paul's rectors have lived here except one. It has become a modern trend for the clergy to invest in homes of their own so in the Spring of 1987 the current rector moved his family to a new home and Preservation Maryland took over the rectory. It will be used for offices and as a lovely setting for parties, receptions, and public meetings. A church person still lives on the third floor.

St. Paul Street Garage in 1930.

18 301 N. Charles Street is the Commercial Credit Annex, designed by Mottu and White and built in 1930. It's a good example of the then popular Art Deco style of architecture. The ground floor contains the works: Bronze and marble doors, fans, chevrons, zigzags, leaf moldings, and doors and screens with a vine motif.[11] Commercial Credit Company bought this building in 1971 and built a low-level walkway to connect with its headquarters on St. Paul Street.

19 Not many people in Baltimore realize that the triangular building on the northwest corner of Charles at Saratoga was the city's first Y.M.C.A. Designed in 1873 by Niersee and Nielson, it was financed by the Garretts and the Browns. It's a heavily decorated mixture of Romanesque and the second Empire Style. When the building was new it was quite flashy with many towers and turrets.

20 Now let's stroll westward to 24 W. Saratoga Street and see the lovely old home on your right. This is the St. Paul's Rectory, built in 1791. It has recently been leased to Preservation Maryland for thirty years and will be restored. It is basically a Federal house. Notice the palladian window over top the front door.

The house was originally one room deep. Rear extensions and other additions were made in 1830 and later.

▶ Baltimore was a major port of entry into America from both Germany and Belgium; hence, it was the most appropriate city in which to have a headquarters for the amazing information system which formed between the American Catholic Church and the international one. St. Alphonsus became the axis for this communication wave. It was staffed by the Redemptorists. At first this order sent missionaries to America in order to convert the Indians. This was a hopeless task and since there were German settlers everywhere, "already in the fold," but without pastors or schools, the Redemptorists changed their American mission.[12]

▶ Marconi's has been an important part of Baltimore since 1920. It's a modest establishment. They don't advertise, but then they don't have to.

Flag House Museum

Star Spangled Banner hung at Park Ave. & Lexington St. in 1927 to raise funds to restore the Flag House.

21 St. Alphonsus Church, designed by Robert Cary Long, Jr. and built in 1845 is on the northeast corner of Saratoga at Park Avenue. In designing the church, Long combined German patterns with English detail and decoration. It's an impressive building with a tower 50 feet taller than the church is long and interesting pointed arch windows. Inside is wonderfully ornate. We suggest you stop in.

Open weekdays 7 am-4 pm. On Thursday there is a Novena which lasts until 6:30 pm. And Sunday the church closes at 12 noon.

22 Marconi's Restaurant is at 106 W. Saratoga Street. It is a favorite for everyone in Baltimore who loves good food and good service. Its decor is unpretentious. They will not take reservations. But do have a meal there if you have the time. You won't regret it. Hours: lunch 12 noon-3:30 pm, dinner 5 pm-8 pm.

Thus ends our tour of the Charles Center Project and its environs. You can walk south to Baltimore Street and the starting point.

Pratt Library

Liberty Street, 1856.

1. Battle Monument
2. Clarence M. Mitchell, Jr. Courthouse
3. Equitable Building
4. Alex Brown and Sons
5. Maryland National Bank Building
6. Continental Building
7. Mercantile Safe Deposit and Trust
8. Marcus Building
9. Chicago bay windows
10. Merchants Club

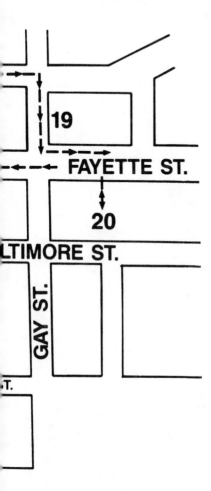

19

FAYETTE ST.

20

LTIMORE ST.

GAY ST.

.T.

11. *Robert Garrett Building*
12. *Furness Building*
13. *Canton Building*
14. *Chamber of Commerce Building*
15. *Gaiety Theatre*
16. *City Hall*
17. *The Peale Museum*
18. *Old Zion Lutheran Church*
19. *War Memorial*
20. *Police Department Headquarters*

THE BALTIMORE FIRE

On Sunday, February 7, 1904 between 10 and 11 am a fire began in a building on Hopkins Place and roared out of control for more than twenty-four hours. When it was finished, the 140 acre area which had been laid out in 1730 and named Baltimore town was rubble. 1,545 buildings had been destroyed. High winds and freezing temperatures had encouraged the fire, but so did the total lack of fire department regulations. This was the commercial and small business section where kerosene, cotton, fertilizer and grain were jammed into warehouses which were immediately adjacent to one another and garment factories, tall buildings, electric wiring, coal and lumber yards were close neighbors.

The Baltimore Fire Department was helpless. Fire fighters came from Washington, Wilmington and Philadelphia but their hoses did not fit the city hydrants. Explosives had to be used and here are several stories about this.

The Baltimore Fire, 1904.

THE BALTIMORE FIRE

The Baltimore Fire, 1904.

Permission to be dynamited had to be granted by the building owner. O'Neill's Department Store stood at the corner of Charles and Lexington one block from the northern perimeter of the fire. Mr. O'Neill refused to have his store blown up. He was a redheaded Irishman who went to the Basilica and told the Lord that if He would save his store O'Neill would see to it that a magnificent cathedral would be built in North Baltimore. Hence was the plan for the Cathedral of Mary Our Queen now on North Charles Street formulated.

William DeFord. It was occupied by Mrs. DeFord and her mother Mrs. Frank Howard, both of whom refused to be evacuated. A shift in the wind saved this section of town from the fire, but the DeFord family will tell you that the fire stopped because the two ladies forbade it to come closer.

We will see some of the buildings which were rebuilt and some of the historic ones which happily remained out of reach of the devestating flames.

▶ No one expected Baltimore to overcome the British in 1814. Excitement was rampant. The decision to build a monument was made by the same committee on Vigilance and Safety that had armed the city against invasion only a few months before. 36 Baltimoreans had been killed. Their names are etched in ribbons along the Monument. There is a bas relief at the base which represents the bombardment of Fort McHenry and the Battle of North Point.

▶ Godefroy was a French engineer who lived in Baltimore from 1809-1819 and who worked as an architect. He donated his drawings but charged the city $800 to supervise its construction.

Calvert Street to the Battle Mounument in 1843.

▶ This block of land was once the center of town. There was a whipping post here, a pillory, and stocks for the public punishment of "evil doers." When the first court house was built, in 1767, the area became known as Court House Hill. The bed for Jones Falls was where Calvert Street is. Ships were anchored where Lexington crosses Calvert. The water was so destructive to the base of the hill that the first court house had to be underpinned by an arch in 1784 and replaced in 1809.[1]

1 Let's begin this tour on Calvert Street beside the Battle Monument. It is the logo for the city and was built to honor the men who died in the 1814 battle of North Point. It is highly allegorical — as such things were supposed to be in those days. The designer was Maximilian Godefroy.

The base is stone with black marble tablets resembling doors and containing inscriptions. There are 18 layers of stone which allude to the 18 constituents of the United States and the doors are replicas of those at the temple of Vesta at Tivoli.

On each corner at the top of the base is a griffin, the symbol of immortality, each with the head of an eagle, the emblem of the United States.

The column is marble 18 feet high to symbolize the Union. The female statue at the top symbolizes Baltimore, wearing a crown of victory and holding a laurel wreath to symbolize glory.[2]

2 The Federal Courthouse. This is the third courthouse to be constructed at this location. It was completed in 1900. The basic steel structure is faced with marble from Beaver Dam on the upper floors. Woodstock granite covers the lower portion.[3] Inside, are rich marbles, mahogany woodwork, and some wonderful murals depicting scenes of early Maryland history. The courthouse is open: Monday-Friday 9 am to 5 pm.

Pratt Library

The Lord Cecil Calvert Monument in 1938.

▶ There are three ghosts who haunt the area. One is Samuel Chase, once a member of the Supreme Court, and a signer of the Declaration of Independence. He may be seen wrapped in a scarlet cloak and wearing a three-cornered hat. Another is a Mrs. Kilburn. She lost her mind while watching her only son stand trial for murder. She roams around the square wearing flowing skirts and carrying a small parasol. A third ghost is Mr. Gallegher. He has a long bushy beard and carries a small satchel. He came to court every day — for years — just to see what was going on. Rumors said he was a real estate person with a fortune in gold inside his satchel. He died here on the hill and his satchel was found to be—empty![4]

▶ In December, 1800 a local paper contained the following announcement:

> The subscriber lately arrived from Ireland has brought with him a complete assortment of 4-4 and 7-8 wide Irish linen which upon inspection will be found lower than any other inspected for three years past, and which will be sold by the box or by the piece for cash or good acceptance in the city on the usual credit. . . .
>
> N.B. He has imported and for sale three dozen very nice mahogany chairs made in the very best construction, and four eight-day clocks which will be sold very low.
>
> Alexander Brown[5]

In order to succeed as a merchant in Maryland a man had to have an instinctive sense for who would buy and sell what overseas, who could be trusted, and a realization that politics, law, and economics were all related. He had to take dramatic risks and roll with the punches. Alexander Brown was a shrewd appraiser of character and he had trusted "spies" in every port with which he dealt. He also was acutely shrewd in his use of credits and currency. His mind turned to banking and he laid the groundwork for what became the first investment banking house in America. He had four sons, one of whom stayed in Baltimore. The others went to company offices in England, Philadelphia, and New York respectively. The business remains in family hands today.

3 At the corner of Calvert and Fayette Streets is the Equitable Building. It was designed by Carson and Speery and was finished in 1894. It was presumed to be fire-proof, but in the Baltimore fire the floors and arches gave way and heavy iron safes fell from the top floors into the basement. It was rebuilt and is considered one of the handsomest commercial-style buildings in the downtown area.

4 Let's stroll south to the corner of Calvert and Baltimore Streets. The warm toned two story brick building on the southwest corner is the bank of Alexander Brown and Sons, the oldest private investment banking house in America. The firm has been located at this spot since 1808. This is its second structure, a nice colonial-revival style, designed by Parker and Thomas, completed in 1900. It is a small two-story building which was constructed to reflect the firm's success, security and prominence. The inside is furnished with rich polished marble, molded plaster detailing, and a magnificent Tiffany style dome, twenty-seven feet in diameter, above the main floor. The dome has recently been cleaned and other aspects of the building have been refurbished. Step in and have a look. It has recently been added to the National Historic Register. It was virtually fireproof because no wood was used in its contruction, but you will note some old scars from the Baltimore fire on the outside wall.

Pratt Library

Alexander Brown Building.

▶ The Safe Deposit Company was organized in 1864 by Enoch Pratt, Henry Walters, S. M. Shoemaker, and Albert Schumacker. These men were concerned with the plight of dependents such as widows, orphans, and the "hopelessly insane" whose fortunes and inheritances were often handled by a "trusted friend." Said friend might abuse this trust and use the monies to his own advantage — or — he might die. In 1876 the Safe Deposit was amended to a "trust company" so that the assets of dependents could be managed and invested by a corporation whose life was permanent and whose dealings were scrupulously honest.[8]

5 Look to the west and you will see The Maryland National Bank Building — one block away. It was designed by Taylor and Fisher and when it was finished in 1929, it was the tallest building in the city (34 floors). Its towers were iced — so to speak — with an exuberance of art deco. Then someone put the initials M.N. around the top to serve as a weather indicator. It spoiled the interesting architecture, but maybe the weather is more important. We must walk eastward, but should you wish to visit the bank building you will see a lovely open lobby, two floors high, with a handsome mosaic floor, an ornate painted ceiling, and multicolored marble columns on the upper level.[6]

6 On the southeast corner of Baltimore and Calvert Streets is the Continental Building designed by D. H. Burnham and Company and finished in 1901 at a cost of $7,000,000. It was the only early building in Baltimore to be built by a Chicago contractor, hence a compromise had to be arranged so that it did not stray too far from the classical form of architecture which was used during that era in downtown Baltimore. The use of triple windows inside each bay and arches, raised several stories in height, are characteristic of the Chicago style.[7] And if you look up the alley as we walk down Redwood Street you will see that the architect put these windows along the back wall. Apparently an act of defiance with the Baltimore style. In 1901, *this* was the tallest building in town (16 floors). It was completely burned out in the Baltimore fire, but its structure was intact and so it was rebuilt. It is now on the National Historic Register.

7 Let's continue south one more block to the corner of Calvert and Redwood. The charming building on the northeast corner is the old Mercantile Safe Deposit and Trust Company, designed in 1885 by Wyatt and Sperry. Notice the "dramatic windows, fine brickwork, and wealth of carved stone detail." This particular style of architecture was used by Stanford White, but it was actually popularized by a western architect named Henry Hobson Richardson and is known as Richardson Romanesque.[7] There are funny little openings along the wall which are called "spy steps." As the cop on the beat made his rounds he would step up and glance into the bank to see that all was well. Baltimore was quite "flush" in the 1880's and this bank was touted as a monument to finance.

▶ Henry Marcus and Sons occupied the building from 1897-1907. They dealt only with wool, supplying it to clothing manufacturers in Baltimore, and exporting it to other states.

▶ The Methodists tended to be very staid in the practice of their religion and for a while they were greatly bothered by music from a dance hall next door to their church. They prayed that the Lord would burn it down. Instead, the hall went for sale and the church was able to buy it and turn it into a college. Then both the church and the college burned to the ground![10]

▶ Robert Garrett, Senior was an Irish merchant who had spent some time in the West and realized its potential. In 1801, he opened a store on Howard Street and began to deal on a reciprocal basis with frontier stores and trade posts. These were established in his name by his agents as new western areas opened up. He sent chalk, chocolate, and tobacco to the west as fast as he could. He received whiskey, snake root, and ginseng in return. He made an enormous fortune which rivaled the Astors and Vanderbilts in New York. His son, Robert, Jr., founded this banking house in 1835. It was the second investment banking firm in America. Another son, John, became the President of the Baltimore and Ohio Railroad and accumulated a vast fortune of his own.

8 Before we turn the corner notice the prim little building at 30 S. Calvert Street. It is known as the Marcus Building and is important because it is one of the few remaining warehouses associated with the era of the clothing industry. The fine detail in the structure of the building indicates a Victorian interest in design and visual attraction regardless of the use to which the building was put. Today, this Marcus Building is part of the inner harbor renaissance. It has been rehabilitated for office and commercial use.

9 As we walk down Redwood Street glance down the alley beside the Mercantile Safe Deposit Company. See the Chicago bay window attached to the back of the Continental Building.

10 206 E. Redwood Street is currently the Merchants Club. The site is the original location for a Methodist Meeting House named the Lovely Lane because it was located on Lovely Lane. It was the first Methodist Episcopal Congregation in the world and stood here from 1774 until 1786. Francis Asbury was elected Bishop here in 1784.

11 233-239 Redwood Street is the Robert Garrett Building designed in 1913 by Wyatt and Nolting. This is an interesting example of early blending of twentieth century architectural simplicity with Victorian Renaissance Revival details. See the design of the windows and the door — clear art and without pretense — as opposed to the central design of doric columns and grillwork. In 1974 the Garrett firm merged with Alexander Brown and Sons. The building has received extensive rehabilitation.

12 The Furness Building at 19-21 South Street was designed in 1917 by a Baltimore architect named Edward Glidden.
Ramsey Scarlett Steamship Managers have had offices here since 1923. The building is an interesting contrast to the larger buildings which surround it.[13] So is the Canton House which is just around the corner at 300 Water Street.

▶ *Prior to the building of Harbor Place, The Block was the attraction which most out-of-towners associated with Baltimore. At one time the burlesque was pretty high class. Entertainers such as Milton Berle and Sophie Tucker were featured here. But during World War II the billing changed to girls and girls and girls. Then there was Blaze Starr, a West Virginia girl (40-24-38) who was also a mistress of Huey Long. She had a club on the Block for years and, she herself was a major attraction. There used to be a man from the Trinity Evangelistic Baptist Church who would play gospel music over loud speaker equipment set up on this very corner. He played every weekend, and sometimes a roving alcoholic would preach a sermon.*[11]

14 On the southeast corner of Water Street and Commerce is the Chamber of Commerce Building, designed by J. R. Niernsee and built in 1880 by the members of the Corn and Flour Exchange. The original building was destroyed in the 1904 fire, but this one is said to be similar. It was rebuilt in 1905.

15 Turn left at Commerce and stroll north to City Hall. Pause a moment at the corner of Baltimore Street. Here Commerce Street becomes Holliday. And here is the western boundary of the Block. It's a smaller area than it used to be, but it is still quite lively. Beer costs a minimum of $1.70 . Whiskey flavored water costs over $3.50. Strippers are still doing their thing. It has always looked pretty seedy in the daytime, but it is seductive and provocative when the lights come on at night.

On your right is the Gaiety Theatre which has been placed on the list of historic properties by the Committee for Historical and Architectural Preservation. It is a monument to burlesque. It will be restored to the grand look it had in the past when its customers knew, as they crossed the elaborate threshold, they would escape to a world much different than the monotonous one they had left behind.

► City Hall was scheduled to be torn down in 1975. It was considered too expensive to maintain. Heating bills were prohibitive. Air conditioning was impossible. There was no space for special offices. Preservationists went into action. Mayor William Donald Schaefer went to Boston to learn what that city had done to save its outdated City Hall. The decision was changed to remodel. This has been expertly accomplished.

City Hall around 1912.

Pratt Library

► Charles Willson Peale was a harness maker and then a silversmith in Annapolis prior to the American Revolution. He showed such potential as a portrait painter that Charles Carroll of Carrollton and Governor Horatio Sharpe sent him to London to study under Benjamin Rush. His first official client was William Pitt.

All of his sons were gifted artists. When Rembrandt Peale built his museum he had gas chandeliers installed — the first in the city — and, because attendance was not good, he inserted the following ad in the local newspaper:

> Will administer Nitrous Oxide for four evenings. When inhaled it produces the highest excitement of which the animal frame is capable. A practical Chemist will administer it. Admission: twenty-five cents. Children: half price.[13]

From 1830-1875 the building was used as Baltimore's City Hall. Then it housed The Bureau of Water Supply, a public school, and a factory. In 1931 it was reopened as a museum.

16 City Hall Square. Look at our City Hall. It's been freshly painted a creamy ivory with a golden dome. A prize of $400.00 was offered in 1870 for the best design and it was won by George A. Frederick, a young man less than twenty years old. The style is based on French origins known as Second Empire Revival and it was designed to rival other post Civil War public buildings which were being constructed at great speed in Washington, D.C. Iron, from Bartlett-Robbins was used as support for the mansard roofs and for the dome. The walls are faced with Beaver Dam marble.[12] Open Monday-Friday 9 am-4 pm. Tours are given daily.

Rembrandt Peale founded the Peale Museum to honor his father, Charles Willson Peale.

17 The Peale Museum was once the old City Hall. The museum was designed by Robert Carey Long, Sr. and was completed in 1814. Rembrandt Peale, the son of Charles Willson Peale, had commissioned the building as a tribute to his father. It was the first municipal museum in the United States.

Today it contains a permanent exhibit of "The Peales: An American Family of Artists." It is open: Tuesday-Saturday 10 am to 5 pm. Sunday 12 noon to 5 pm. Admission fee.

Pratt Library

Charles Willson Peale.

▶ The first directory of Baltimore Towne, published in 1796, showed 10 per cent of the names listed were German:[14] The Zion Church was the center of all social and religious activities of the German Lutherans. It was also a pioneer in the education of children. "It is an uncontestable fact that a good education lays the foundation to our future happiness," said Dr. Charles Frederick Wicsenthal in 1800.

▶ Note that the paving pattern in the City Hall Plaza is intended to symbolize graves.

18 The Old Zion Lutheran Church, designed by Rehrback and Machenheimer, was built in 1807. These two men were carpenters who had worked with Maximilian Godefroy when he built the St. Mary's Seminary Chapel. The pointed windows and battlements are similar. The stained glass windows are among the finest in the city and the garden is one of the nicest places to rest in the heart of Baltimore. There are some interesting old tiles which depict stories of the Bible and two of the early rectors are buried here. The church is open every day. Phone 685-3939 to plan a tour.

19 The War Memorial, designed by Lawrence Fowler, was built 1921-1923 to honor World War I heroes. The sea horses on the sides of the steps are intended to represent the marines. Records of every Marylander who participated in World War I and World War II are stored in this building. There is an interesting mural by Macgill Mackill, a Baltimore artist, on the west wall of the second floor and some interesting exhibits on the first floor level. You are welcome to browse. Open: Monday-Friday 9 am-4 pm.

NOTES Downtown Baltimore

▶ This section was once the center of Baltimore Towne. The Holliday Street Theater stood where the plaza is today. It was finished in 1813, a year before the Peale, and it was here the "Star Spangled Banner" was first sung. The song was so stirring that the audience asked for it night after night. Edwin Booth, the father of John Wilkes Booth and a famous interpreter of Shakespeare, played in the theater every winter.

▶ The Baltimore Assembly was on the northeast corner of Fayette and Holliday. This was a snazzy club which opened in 1798. Betsy Patterson brought her beaux here to dances and here a Special Silver Supper was served to Lafayette. John H. B. Latrobe described the hall. . . . "there is a card room which later became a supper room for gentlemen. Here the men may at their ease indulge the gothic practice of cramming themselves with comestibles without fair eyes to gaze at them."[15]

20 601 E. Fayette Street is the Police Department Headquarters. It was designed by Fenton and Lichtig and opened in August, 1972. The front lobby contains seven wonderful murals by Baltimore artist Joseph Sheppard. There is a museum to the right of the entrance which has a display of many early restraints, police uniforms, and even an original paddy wagon.

There is a heliport on the roof from which the helicopters which survey the city come and go.

The building is open Monday-Friday 8:30 am to 4:30 pm. Tours may be arranged by calling 396-2012.

This ends our tour, let's turn east on Fayette Street and return to the Battle Monument.

Pratt Library

The Battle Monument in 1894.

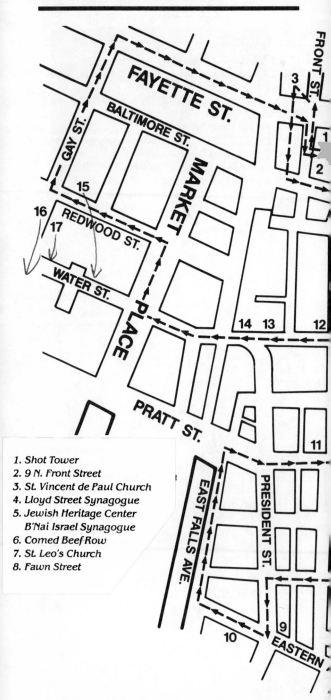

1. Shot Tower
2. 9 N. Front Street
3. St. Vincent de Paul Church
4. Lloyd Street Synagogue
5. Jewish Heritage Center
   B'Nai Israel Synagogue
6. Corned Beef Row
7. St. Leo's Church
8. Fawn Street

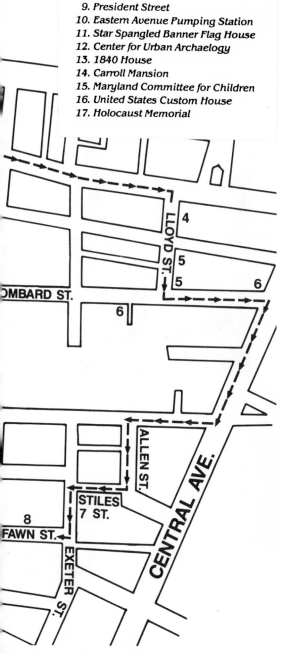

NOTES Downtown Baltimore

▶ There were once three such towers in Baltimore. Charles Carroll of Carrollton laid the cornerstone for this one in 1828.

Fayette Street looking west, 1935.

▶ Thorowgood Smith was a merchant who fell on hard times. He had built a handsome country house named "Willowbrook" near what is now Union Square, but he was never able to move in because his ships were seized by alien forces and he was obliged to declare bankruptcy. From 1804-1808 he served as the second mayor of Baltimore. He was a vain man, who wore his glasses on a ribbon around his forehead so he would not mar the surface of his elegant nose. But he served the city well: laid the foundations for the establishment of a city police department, encouraged the passing of the first ordinance to bring water into the city, and voted to allow the Baltimore Water Company to lay conduit pipes.

1 Shot Tower Park. Contrary to appearances, the shot tower was not a fortification. It was used literally for the making of shot. "Molten lead was poured in drops from the top. It formed into balls as it fell, and solidified upon hitting cold water at the bottom," thereupon becoming shot. The structure is 234 feet tall and was once known as The Phoenix Shot Tower. The foundation walls are 17 féet thick. The diameter is 40½ feet at the base and tapers to 20 feet at the top.[1] There is an informative audiovisual recording inside plus an interesting exposition of the interior of such towers. Step in and have a look.

2 9 Front Street is a charming 18th century town house. Notice the large windows and the unusually distinctive chimney. There is a fireplace in every room. The house was built about 1790 and was, for two years, the home of Thorowgood Smith when he became Mayor of Baltimore. It has been a hotel, an apartment house, and a second hand auto parts shop. In 1972 it was rented by the city for a dollar a year to the Women's Civic League who restored it to be used as their headquarters thus saving it from demolition. It is open:

Tuesday-Saturday: 10 am-4 pm
Sunday: 12 noon to 4 pm

Tourists are invited in. Information relating to the city is available.

T. Chandlee

9 Front Street.

▶ *Front Street was once the most fashionable street in town. There was a theater at the corner of Front and Fayette Streets where Jenny Lind sang in December, 1850 and Abraham Lincoln was nominated for his second term in office. Notices for the Lind concert read:*

> Doors open at six. Concert will begin at eight....The choice seats will be disposed of at an auction at the theater on December seventh.

There was a terrible traffic jam the night of the concert. Every seat was taken. When Miss Lind appeared "the whole house rose...and rapturous tokens of appreciation compelled her to repeat two of her numbers... habited in pink satin she sang "Home Sweet Home" and the audience wept unashamedly."[2]

▶ *The Lincoln Convention was held here because Baltimore was close to Washington. It was wild. "Friend refused to speak to friend: and brother spat at brother" because there were many confederate rebels here. The Maryland Club, which was then located at the corner of Franklin and Cathedral Streets, was considered to be the focus of treason by the Federalists. But inside the theater the band from Fort McHenry played the Star Spangled Banner. There were many speeches, "the wildest excitement was provoked by Lincoln's name. He was unanimously chosen to be the Republican candidate."[3]*

· AUTO TOPS

3 Across Fayette Street, St. Vincent de Paul Church is a slight deviation from the rest of the tour, but we love this old church. It always seems so bright and freshly painted: white and green, and stands undiscouraged by the myriad of changes which have taken place around it. It was designed and built in 1841 by its first pastor, The Reverend John B. Gildea. Notice the wonderful three-tiered tower, topped by a dome and a cross. It was built at a time when there was great rivalry and concurrent jealousy between the Irish and the German elements of the Catholic Church. There was a school connected with the church which was run by the Brothers of Christian Schools. It had 500 students, a number equalled only by St. Peter the Apostle School which was located in the area adjacent to the railroad shops in southwest Baltimore. The church is open from:

10 am-12 noon Monday-Friday

Tours may be arranged by calling 962-5078.

Now let's walk back across Front Street to Baltimore Street and turn left. This is the neighborhood in which Baltimore's Jewish Community has its roots. It was settled in the early to mid 1800's by German Bavarian Jews who were well educated and anxious to succeed in the new homeland. Turn right at Lloyd Street.

▶ By 1880, the original settlers in this area had made their fortunes and were ready to move uptown. They built the magnificent Eutaw Place neighborhood and moved into it. At the same time, there was an influx of Jewish refugees from Russia. Many of them crowded into these houses which had just been vacated. They created an enormous problem. They knew nothing about American mores, could not speak English, and could not deal with the currency. They were quite willing to work, but the economy was in a depression. Henrietta Szold organized what is generally considered to be the original immigrant night school at Baltimore and Asquith Streets. Seven thousand attended its classes.[4]

▶ The phenomenon of the sweat shop developed. There were three to four hundred of them on Lombard Street east to Central Avenue. This was the heart of the clothing worker's industry. Six to eight persons would cut, baste or sew in a room which measured 10'x12'. Seated at work tables these people worked 16 hours a day, six days a week for a pittance. Often the sweat shop would be on the third floor with living arrangements behind it and another business such as a bakery below it.[5] The problem ended when the large clothing factories were opened on Pratt, Eutaw, and Greene Streets.

▶ Many of these stores originally sold kosher food and imported delicacies. There was a time when the street seemed like one big smorgasbord. People strolled casually around, eating, drinking, and visiting with one another.

Currently business comes from government offices and downtown businesses which "send out" for lunch. Both Attman's and Jack's have catering services for old time Jewish food such as lox and bagels plus a large selection of other dishes.

4 Lloyd Street Synagogue, built in 1845 was the first synagogue in Maryland and the third in the United States. It was designed by Robert Cary Long, Sr. for the Baltimore Hebrew Society. In 1950 it was scheduled to be replaced by a filling station. The Jewish Historical Society moved quickly to buy the property and it is now a museum.

It is open for tours the first and third Sunday of each month 1:30-4 pm.

T. Chandlee

Lloyd Street Synagogue.

5 Next door is the Jewish Heritage Center which opened in 1986, and on the corner is B'nai Israel Synagogue, built in 1875 and still in use. It's a lovely building and can be seen at the same hours as the Lloyd Street Synagogue, the first and third Sunday of every month 1:30-4 pm.

Other times may be arranged by phoning 732-6400.

6 The 1000 block of Lombard Street is known as corned beef row. We must stop at Attman's (1019) or Jack's (east on the corner) of Lombard Street and Central Avenue for a warm corned beef on rye and a kosher pickle. If you decide to make it Attman's, look at the counter for an interesting candy named halvah. The recipe is 5,000 years old! Try a piece.

▶ It would be difficult to recommend a restaurant in Little Italy. Shop around yourself. Some are less expensive than others. There are a variety of house specialities. Find what you like and revel in it.

▶ Italians began to come to Baltimore from Genoa in the early 1800's, but the majority appear to have come here from New York in the 1850's when the railroad began to run. The gold rush was on in the west and these people thought they would be able to hitch a ride west on the B&O. They couldn't unless they paid for it, so they settled here and found jobs as cooks, laborers, tailors, barbers, and organ grinders. A man named Merici lived on the northeast corner of Eastern Avenue and President Street. His home was the headquarters for the hurdy-gurdy men. For years, Italians with street pianos, fiddles, dancing bears on a leash, and a monkey who tipped his hat when you gave him a penny, were confirmation of the advent of Spring in Baltimore.

▶ The family and the home is very important to the Italian. Many came to America with plans to make a fortune, return to Italy, buy land and build a home. Some actually did this. Others became burdened with family obligations on this continent and could not afford to leave. How fortunate!

▶ Railroading in this section began with horsecars and graduated to British locomotives which were already obsolete in 1835, but had been imported to run from President Street to Port Deposit. The line later became part of the Philadelphia, Wilmington, and Baltimore. Fights in the city council went on for years and each related to the problem of efficient hauls from this President Street Station to the one named Camden. Pratt Street was the connecting link. Passengers could walk the few blocks, but freight had to be conveyed by car through the "streets of bustle."[7] Should this car be pushed by laborers, pulled by horse, or propelled by steam?

7 We'll walk down Central Avenue for one block and turn east on Stiles. This is another ethnic neighborhood known as Little Italy. We're going to the corner of Exeter Street and Stiles to visit St. Leo's Church. If you ring the bell at the rectory, the priest will let you into the church.

For many years the closest church in this area was St. Vincent de Paul. The buoyant Italians rebelled at being forced to comply with Anglican reserve. They were told to sit in the balcony and were not encouraged to participate in many of the church activities. They pled with Cardinal Gibbons until he agreed to let them have a church of their own. St. Leo's was designed by Francis Baldwin and built in 1880. It is a warm, elaborate church with Tiffany glass in its windows and a marvelous canvas full of angels under the dome.

8 Fawn Street is one whose appearance most personifies the mores of Little Italy. Notice that there are plastic flowers and a Holy Figure in nearly every window. Such a display is really a continuum of early Italian customs as this group sought to become established in a new homeland. They are left behind as a new generation becomes "Americanized" and moves "up town."

9 President Street and Easten Avenue. A block to your left is the remnant of the prestigious President Street Station, built in 1850. The major portion was burned years ago, but it was here, on April 19, 1861, that Union troops disembarked and began their march down Pratt Street toward Camden Station on the way to Washington to answer a call for help from President Lincoln. They were attacked by Southern sympathizers and twelve were killed. This was the first blood to be shed in the incipient War between the States.

T. Chandlee

Sisters Rose Lamm and Grace Flack at home in Little Italy.

▶ In the eighteenth century, flag making was one of the acceptable occupations for women. The flag which inspired Francis Scott Key was larger than the ordinary and was put together by Mrs. Pickersgill in a building on Lombard Street. The Americans had not expected to win the Battle at Fort McHenry so when the British ships departed local relief was intense. The triumphant tone of the Key poem made it an instant success. It was set to the tune of a popular song "Anacreon in Heaven", but it was hard to sing. "My Country T'is of Thee" (whose tune is the same as the British anthem "God Save the Queen") and "America the Beautiful" were often played to represent this country when patriotism was needed.

There was no official national anthem until 1931. Congress had determined that we needed one and

10 The Eastern Avenue Sewage Pumping Station, built in 1912, contains part of Baltimore's original sewage system and is an interesting place to visit. This is an ornate Victorian building with a copper trimmed roof that is handsome in spite of its pedestrian function."[6] Walk past the front entrance and turn left. The southwest section of the building contains a museum which features the historical beginnings of all the services we take for granted in our everday life: water, trash removal, sewer service, road maintenance and street lighting. It is the nation's first Public Works Museum and fascinating to see. Hours are:

Phone: 396-5565
Wednesday-Sunday 11 am to 5 pm.

11 Now we'll stroll up Falls Avenue to Pratt Street and turn east. At 844 is the Star Spangled Banner Flag House, built in 1793. It was the home and flag making establishment of Rebecca Young who made flags for some of George Washington's regiments during the American Revolution. In 1813, her daughter Mary Pickersgill was hired to make the huge flag which flew over Fort McHenry during the British bombardment in 1814 and which inspired the writing of our National anthem. The house is furnished and there is a museum which commemorates the War of 1812. It is open:

Monday-Saturday 10 am-4 pm
Sunday 1 pm-4 pm
Admission fee

Mary Pickersgill who made the flag which flew over Ft. McHenry.

MD Historical Society

debates were begun. A local women, Mrs. Reuben Ross Holloway, was a force behind Congressman Charles J. Linthicum who introduced the bill which became law making "The Star Spangled Banner" the official anthem. Mrs. Holloway was short. She had a wardrobe of hats, each was exactly one foot high. The color and trimming might change but the shape never did. When the decision regarding the anthem became official, Mrs. Holloway regarded the flag as her personal charge, and she handed out certificates of merit to business, houses and institutions which displayed it in the proper manner.[8]

Ft. McHenry

Mrs. Reuben Ross Holloway champion for the "Star Spangled Banner."

Flag House Museum

Carling painting of Mary Pickersgill finishing the Star Spangled Banner.

12 Let's go north on Albemarle Street for one block. At the corner of Lombard and Albemarle is the Center for Urban Archaeology which has been in existence since 1983. Inside you will hear how old privy sites can provoke ecstacy in the hearts of archeologists.

13 We'll turn west onto Lombard Street. The 1840 house is a reconstructed 19th century row house which was once the home of John Hutchinson, a wheelwright. There is a program of "hands-on" activities and an attempt to recreate life as it was lived when this little home was new. Admission is by the gate in the alley beside 800 E. Lombard. Admission fee.

Charles Carroll, signer of the Declaration of Independence.

▶ *The factory was rehabilitated in such good taste by the Maryland Committee for Children that they won an award in 1980 from Baltimore Heritage, Inc.*

The Custom House.

14 800 E. Lombard Street was built about 1812. It is an excellent example of Federal style architecture as well as an elegant town house which is currently furnished with the Empire-style decorations of the period. Charles Carroll of Carrollton wintered here with his family during his final years (1820-1832.) The house fell on hard times during the commercialization of Baltimore City. It was a saloon, a tenement, a factory warehouse and a furniture store. Then it became the city's first vocational school and a recreation center. Happily now it is back to what it was intended to be. Enter through the gate in the alley beside the house.
  Open Tuesday-Sunday 10 am-4 pm.
  Admission fee.

Note the large building across the Fallsway to the left. This is the Candler Building built in 1915 to be a bottling plant for the Coca Cola Company. It has since been converted to offices.

15 We're going to go up Market Place to Water Street and walk one block east to Gay Street. 608 Water Street is called the Chocolate Factory, because it was one of the city's first chocolate factories built in 1910 after the first building was destroyed in the fire. It is currently owned by the city and rented to The Maryland Committee for Children. Stop in and visit their re-STORE.
  Open Monday-Friday 10 am-5 pm.
  Saturday 10 am-2 pm.

16 The United States Custom House was designed by Hornblower and Marshall in 1907. The style is known as "Beaux Arts" and is distinguished by the three-story engaged columns, the triangular pediment over the third story windows, and the rooftop balustrade. Inside, on the first floor, is a "call room" which contains a 30-by-60 foot ceiling canvas titled "Entering Port." There are also smaller paintings titled "The History of Navigation." All are by Francis Davis Millet and said by experts to be the "finest decorative art in any building in the country."[10]
  Open Monday-Friday 9 am-5 pm.

NOTES Downtown Baltimore

▶ *Some curious underground passages were uncovered when excavations were made for the Custom House. Inside some of the passages were skeletons. It seems there was once a hotel on Water Street with a wonderful cuisine which was managed by a Frenchman whose home was directly behind the hotel. He had a wife and children who were not allowed in the inn. Rumors were that some of the people who stopped at the inn were never seen again. One night, the wife sneaked in, hid in the cupboard, and saw her husband murder a client and take his money. She left him. His victims were not found until 1900.*[9]

▶ *Prior to the Custom House there was a lovely building designed by B. H. Latrobe, built in 1820, and known as the Merchant's Exchange. It contained a custom house and it was the place where Lincoln's body lay in state in Baltimore. Next door to the Exchange were the warehouses belonging to Johns Hopkins and to Henry Walters.*

Pratt Library

Exchange Place, 1868.

The Baltimore Exchange building, 1852.

17 On the southeast corner of Gay Street at Water is a monument to the Holocaust, commissioned by the Jewish Council of Baltimore and dedicated in November, 1980. It was designed by Donald Kann, a Baltimore architect, and Arthur D. Falk, a local sculptor. Together with two giant monoliths there are six rows of pear trees which symbolize the six million Jews killed by the Nazi Germans.

We'll continue north on Gay Street to Fayette and back to 9 Front Street.

The Holocaust Memorial.

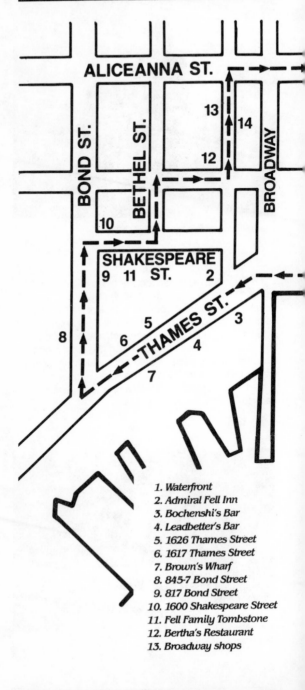

1. Waterfront
2. Admiral Fell Inn
3. Bochenshi's Bar
4. Leadbetter's Bar
5. 1626 Thames Street
6. 1617 Thames Street
7. Brown's Wharf
8. 845-7 Bond Street
9. 817 Bond Street
10. 1600 Shakespeare Street
11. Fell Family Tombstone
12. Bertha's Restaurant
13. Broadway shops

14. *Broadway Market*
15. *St. Stanislaus Church*
16. *700 block Ann Street houses*
17. *800 block Ann Street houses*
18. *802 S. Ann Street*
19. *Robert Long House*
20. *Captain Pitt House*
21. *Captain John Steele House*
22. *Belt's Wharf*
23. *933 S. Wolfe Street*
24. *914 S. Wolfe Street*
25. *1815 Thames Street*
26. *1738 Thames Street*

▶ In 1730 William Fell bought a tract of land known as Copus Harbor and built a mansion on it. The southern border of that tract of land is known as Thames Street today.

▶ The shipyards, wharves, and adjoining warehouses were not begun until other settlers arrived at the Point in the mid 1700's. Most of them were Quakers. They built sturdy houses using a modish style of brick laying known as Flemish bond.

▶ There is a lingering sense of the village which was begun when William Fell divided his property into lots and lined up new streets with the water front. He named these streets from the ones he knew in London: Philpot, Thames, Fell and Bond.

▶ The city bricked the plaza and the sidewalks when it realized how popular Fells Point had become to visitors.

1 This tour begins at the foot of Broadway, near Thames Street.

Face the waterfront, see the tug boats and hear the noises of the port. The U.S. Frigate Constellation, first ship to be commissioned by the U.S. Navy was built here. So were 60 more Navy frigates and also the famous Baltimore Clipper ships. Do you see any sails on the horizon?

Now turn and look at the houses which line the foot of Broadway, These are 17th and 18th century houses with slanted roofs and wide chimneys.

Fells Point is a unique 18th century neighborhood which contains an active port, the original town plan, and most of the original architecture. It was rescued from total destruction in 1965 by an infinite labor of love on the part of a handful of people.

Pratt Library

Baltimore Harbor in 1947 by A.A. Bodine

2 The Admiral Fell Inn. From 1892-1955 this was a seaman's boarding house known as the Anchorage. It has recently been remodeled into one of Baltimore's most attractive regional Inns.

The Vagabond Theater is home for an amateur theater group which has been in Baltimore for more than fifty years. Mildred Natwick and Zelda Fitzgerald are two who have starred here. Their forte is very good revivals of old plays.

▶ The name Broadway is a literal one: meaning broad way. In the days when clipper ships were launched here there was a rope walk in the middle of the street which stretched from the docks to Aliceanna Street. Strands of rope which were to become cables for these ships were placed along this walk and a ropemaker walked its length twisting the rope as he went with a hand wrench.

▶ The side streets in Fells Point have retained their original narrow widths. Most of the houses were the homes of seamen and dockworkers.

Pratt Library

200 to 300 S. Broadway showing above ground telephone wires and electric company poles.

▶ As the port developed so did the land adjacent to it. Broadway grew northward, lined with homes of ship's captains, physicians, brewers, and, of all things, butchers! More about that later.

3 Let's start down Thames Street. Stop for a moment at 1643. Note the name J. R. Bochenshi embedded in the front stoop. Go inside and look. Beside the bar is a copper spittoon which runs the length of the bar along the floor in front of the stools. Have you ever seen one like it?

4 1639 Thames is a bar which is frequented by college students and young professional people. The name — Leadbetters — is the name of a beer parlor which was here for many years.

5 1626 Thames was built by a Captain Forbes in the 1700's.

6 1618 Thames. Note the row of houses which begins here. They were built on an angle in order to conform to the lot lines. The roofs, in the rear, have interesting hull-like shapes. They were built by seamen who had no architectural experience. Research indicates that the Fell Mansion was in this area.

7 1617 Thames is Brown's Wharf. This is an 1822 warehouse which was built for Alexander Brown. It is now a private museum with an excellent collection of ship's models and other Fells Point memoribilia. It is open by appointment only. Phone: 276-1013.

8 Turn right onto Bond Street. The 1795 newspaper office which printed the Fells Point Telegraph three times a week was located in this block.

Notice the nice cornice which connects 845 to 847 Bond Street.

9 817 Bond Street was built in 1876 to be a hotel and dance hall. This is the second such structure on this site. It has recently been converted into apartments.

830 Bond Street was built by Captain John Winning about 1782. The lot was originally on the water. It is thought that the first hospital in Baltimore was housed here.

1628 to 1632 Shakespeare Street prior to restoration.

► *In the early 1960's, certain politicians were determined that this area would be destroyed to make way of Interstate 83. I will list certain events which occurred:*

1. Summer, 1965. A condemnation hearing was held in downtown Baltimore in order that most of Fells Point could be made available for a new east-west highway.

2. A small group of preservationists set out to abort this plan. In April, 1966, this group went to the Federal Highway Administration in Washington D.C. with a plea to save Fells Point.

3. Summer, 1967. Volunteers did a house to house survey of five essential blocks in Fells Point in order to document the architectural aspects of each house and to detail its historical importance.

4. October, 1967. Officials from the Department of Interior, including its secretary, reviewed the survey and toured Fells Point.

10 Turn right onto Shakespeare Street. 1600 Shakespeare Street was built by John Smith in 1773. Its ground rent is still payable in shillings!

11 A tombstone marks the grave of the Fell family. For many years there was no marker. People were told that the Bard himself was buried here and they believed it!

12 Let's turn left at Bethel Street. Walk a block to Lancaster. Turn right. Bertha's Restaurant, best known for fresh mussels, is on the corner. The owners are Scottish musicians who frequently have chamber music in the second floor dining room. High tea is served on Wednesday from 3-5 pm. Stop in if you have the time.

13 Lower Broadway Shops. Many of these are a trifle "off beat" but do browse in them. There are treasures to be found.

Pratt Library

1600 Shakespeare Street.

5. *1968. A citizen's suit against construction of the highway was filed. By this time, the support of hundreds of Baltimoreans had been gained.*

6. *1969. Fells Point was listed in the National Register of Historic Places and was among the first in the nation to be designated as a Federal Historic District. This made the spending of Federal monies to demolish historic property illegal.*

7. *Plans to re-route the east-west highway were finally made official.*

▶ *Rehabilitation of these houses has been sporadic. The city threatened to reclaim those which were not refurbished by 1984. This put a "hurry-up" on the laggards so that rehabilitaton of this particular section is complete.*

▶ *The area is a melting pot. Many of the oldest residents are Greek, Italian and Polish shopkeepers who bitterly resented the preservationists. There was a second fight — following the one with the States Road Commission. The old residents were afraid they were going to be forced to live in "a museum." They did not understand the restriction laws which controlled changes to building facades. They resented being told what they could and could not do with their property. Time has helped them to "cool it." They love the influx of visitors and the new business they are getting.*

▶ *The city of Baltimore owned only 70 of the houses which were bought by preservationists. The rest of the houses were on the private market. The city was able to use and to enforce the same standards for restoration which it used in the Otterbein area i.e. the houses it sold **had** to be restored to their original outside appearance and the buyer had to live in it six months after it was purchased. There was no controlling body for the other houses. The Society for the Preservation of Federal Hill and Fells Point did its best to encourage buyers to stick to early forms of architecture. Neighbors, too, had their say. It is plain to see that not all of Fells Point has been restored. No one knows what the future will bring.*

14 The Broadway Market was built in 1784 on land allotted for a market by Edward Fell. Its construction identified Broadway as a commercial street so taverns, lodging houses, stables, blacksmiths, and harness makers soon surrounded it. There were originally four markets here. Now there are two. They have recently been restored. Many of the vendors know a lot about the Point so do wander through them both.

Pratt Library

The Old Broadway Market.

15 Let's walk east on Aliceanna Street to Ann Street. This was once a vibrant Polish neighborhood. 702-724 S. Ann Street is the St. Stanislaus Kostka Church. This is the oldest Roman Catholic congregation established in Baltimore by and for Polish emigrees. It was built in 1889 by refugees from Bismarck. Its parishioners met in a rented house at the corner of Bond and Fleet Streets for twelve years while their church was being built. It's a lovely Gothic church, well worth a visit inside. Tours may be arranged by calling: 276-2849.

16 717 and 719 S. Ann Street are late 18th century frame buildings and predate the building code which prohibited this type of housing because of its propensity to fire.

▶ A wonderful collection of clay pipes and other artifacts were unearthed while 802 S. Ann was being restored. It is felt that there may once have been a club or meeting house on the premises.

L.H. Fowler

Fell Street in 1914.

▶ Robert Long was a carpenter by trade and was one of the earliest settlers in Fells Point. Some say it was he who influenced William Fell to block off his land and to lay the foundations for the village which grew here.

▶ The Captain Steele house has been beautifully restored by the family who bought it in 1967 and who lived in it while they did their renovation work. (Many people thought they should have their heads examined. Fell Street was slum.) It has a beautiful original arch by the stairway, which the Metropolitan Museum of Art tried to buy. It contains six original fireplaces and a lovely balustrade winding from the first to the fourth floor. Notice the fanlight over the door.

17 801 and 803 S. Ann Street are typical 19th century houses. The land was leased by William Fell to Jeremiah Andrews, a Philadelphia gold-smith and jeweler, in 1782.

18 802 S. Ann Street was restored by the owners of Bertha's Restaurant. It was built about 1800 by a ship's captain. Note the small attachment on the roof. This was called a penthouse and was built to be used as a fire escape.

Interior of the Robert Long House.

19 812 S. Ann Street was built about 1765 by Robert Long. It is the oldest urban house in Baltimore. It has recently been restored and is the headquarters for the Society for the Preservation of Federal Hill and Fell's Point.

There is no other house in Baltimore like it although the style is common in Philadelphia. The roof is known as a shed dormer and there is a water table which stores rain water and throws away the excess during storms. The only way to learn more about this house is to step inside. Phone: 675-6750. Admission fee.

20 We'll cross Thames Street and stroll down Fell Street. 910 is the Captain Pitt house, built about 1790. The exterior has been greatly altered, but inside is quite intact. Restoration work uncovered three levels of brick floors and some wonderful wide brick arches in the ceiling.

Pratt Library

The William Fell House in 1936.

▶ The recreation pier on the left was opened August 20, 1914. It was built by the city at a cost of $1,000,000. During World War I the Baltimore Chapter of the Daughters of 1812 began to chaperone bi-weekly dances for soldiers, but its members refused to participate because they felt that the neighborhood girls were a bad influence on the men. "They even take the soldiers to their homes!" they said with raised eyebrows.

The dances went on anyway. Local parents chaperoned their daughters and were glad to welcome the boys into their homes.

▶ The pier was also used for classes in English during its first years. It had a library and there was a playground for children on the roof.

It is still owned by the city. Today there are offices in the pier and parking spaces where boats used to be put into dry dock.

21 931 is the Captain John Steele house, built about 1790. It was originally free-standing and is about the best example of Federal architecture still standing in Baltimore.

22 Belt's Wharf Warehouses are more than 115 years old. The company still handles almost all of the green coffee coming into the port today.

23 933 S. Wolfe Street was once a cannery— built in 1836 to handle oysters and, later, fruits and vegetables brought in from the Eastern Shore. There are plans to convert these abandoned buildings into harborside apartment dwellings.

24 914 S. Wolfe Street was originally a pair of working class houses built in the early 1800's. They were placed at a 45° angle to the street so that the house could have a square front.

25 We'll turn left at the corner of Wolfe Street at Thames and walk westward. 1815 Thames Street was originally two houses. It was restored at the same time as the Steele house—in 1967. There is an interesting staircase of long grain pine which was brought from a colonial home in Delaware.

The inside is not too authentic, but it is attractive.

26 1738 E. Thames Street is the River Drive Inn. This was a very early tavern. Notice the attic dormers, hip roof, and wooden cornice.

And here we are . . . at the point from which we started.

Stop in one of the bars and have a drink. They each have atmosphere.

NOTES East Baltimore

A. *St. Patrick's Church*
B. *American Indian Study Center*
C. *Holy Cross Polish National Church*
D. *Olde Obrycki's Crab House*
E. *Washington Hill*
F. *4 S. Broadway*
G. *Citizens of Washington Hill, Inc.*
H. *Drugstore*
1. *Ferinand Latrobe Monument*
2. *Church Hospital*
3. *Thomas Wildey Monument*
4. *"Paestum"*
5. *The Johns Hopkins Hospital*
6. *Hampton House*
7. *John F. Kennedy Institute*
8. *Turner Auditorium*
9. *Welch Medical Library*
10. *School of Public Health and Hygiene*
11. *Henry Phipps Clinic*
12. *Old Hospital Laundry*
13. *Housing project*

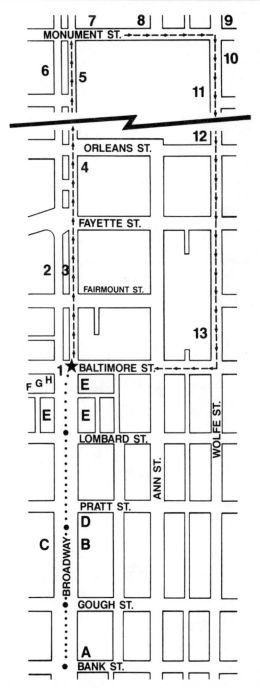

▶ *The original French Catholics were joined by French refugees from Santo Domingo. The French called themselves "gentlemen," a rather ambiguous title in early America, but they did add a touch of style to the life here. They introduced hairdressing, millinery, perfumery, music, dancing, and fencing, plus political and religious ferment, croissants, and patisseries. The first St. Patrick's was a famous landmark in early Baltimore. Every winter, three stoves were placed in the aisles, making it the first heated church in Baltimore.*

Father James N. Dolan became the parish priest in 1841. 1847 was the year of the famine in Ireland. Many of those who fled were so weak that they died of ship's fever at sea, but their children survived. Father Dolan set up a house for orphans next door to the church and built a school for boys. In 1870, he willed money for a Free School and a Children's Aid Society—so St. Patrick's became the first public school in the State of Maryland and one of the first parochial schools in the United States.[1]

T. Chandlee

The Indian Center.

This is not the best of areas to walk in so we mention spots of interest and then we will begin the tour in a northern section.

A St. Patrick's Church at Broadway and Bank Streets. The parish was established in 1792 and is the oldest existing Catholic parish in Baltimore. No one can tell you why the church was named for the great Irish Saint because the first pastor and most of the early parishioners were French. It has a marvelous history.

The present church replaced the original in 1897. It has just been repaired after a devastating fire in August, 1983.

It may be visited by phoning the parish office: 675-0640.

B 211 S. Broadway is the American Indian Study Center. We have a tribe of Indians in Baltimore named the Lumbees. Some think they may be descended from the Lost Colony at Roanoke. There are 3,000-4,000 with a sprinkling of Cherokee, Sioux, and Blackfoot. They were brought to public attention when the Butchers Hill area was vacated in readiness for restoration. The Indians were living on welfare and had a myriad of social problems. The Center has been in existence about 10 years. It has been remarkably successful in rehabilitating its clients. It has recently opened a gift shop with an inventory of Indian crafts from the west. The stock includes moccasins, earthenware and silver jewelry. Open daily except Sunday.

C 208 S. Broadway is Holy Cross Polish National Church, organized in 1898 after long standing turmoil between the Polish-American community and the Irish dominated Archdiocese of Baltimore.

The interior is an interesting one of early baroque design, a triple barrel vault ceiling, corinthian capitals, carved wooden altar, pulpit and statues.
Phone 327-8229 for admission.

▶ Several years ago, Craig Claiborne organized a group in New York to come to eat at Obrycki's. They returned the same night and he wrote a column about it for the New York Times.

▶ There were dreadful epidemics of yellow fever and other diseases transmitted by flies and mosquitoes around the harbor area. Medical methods for dealing with these problems were not very sophisticated.

▶ John Hall's pattern book, Modern Designs, published in 1840 contained a variety of plans for row houses. Every plan could be scaled up or down, depending upon the size of the house and the pocket book of the builder. The book had a major influence on Baltimore builders. In the 1850's parlors became very important. Large houses had double ones, with a dining room and a kitchen behind. Ceilings were high. Mantles were marble and gas light was becoming universal. Cast iron lintels, fences, and balconies were growing popular.

These homes were built for those who could afford to escape the harbor.

▶ In 1942, many people moved to Baltimore from Tennessee and the Carolinas to work in defense plants. These Broadway houses were converted into multiple dwelling units to house them. Thus began their ultimate deterioration. By 1970 this was a slum area and the city had plans to clear it.

D 1729 Pratt Street (just around the corner from Broadway) is Olde Obrycki's Crab House, known nationally for its crab dishes. The building was once a tavern. We think you will enjoy stopping in. It is open April-October. Tuesday-Friday, 11:30-2:30 pm; Saturday, 5 pm-11 pm; Sunday, 4 pm-9 pm. Phone 732-6399 for reservations.

E Washington Hill is the section north of Lombard Street. It was farm land until after the Civil War. Then sea captains began to build homes here.

The house on the southeast corner of Broadway and Baltimore Street was built about 1840 for the Thomas Hugg family. It has recently been restored and is now cooperative apartments.

F 4 S. Broadway was also built about 1840. When it was restored a few years ago, the ruins of a conservatory were found in its side yard.

G 2 S. Broadway is the headquarters for the Citizens of Washington Hill, Inc. Washington Hill includes some blocks east and west of here.

H The drug store on the corner of Broadway and Baltimore Streets is said to be the oldest one in the city. There is a new shop-steading area around the corner in the 1600 block of Baltimore Street. You might like to check it out.

▶ *The practice of medicine was suspect in those days. Here is an excerpt from the diary of a citizen of the time:*

Before this college was built, doctors had a hard time trying to find their patient's trouble. If an operation was proposed by a doctor, nine times out of ten it would not be allowed by the patient. Doctors were not in many cases successful, which made the public dread operations, and they would rather die than let a doctor operate on them. Often when a person died and a doctor wanted the body, he would get grave robbers to get the dead body which would be buried in the day and be delivered to the doctor's office in the dead of night. The cost would be about ten dollars to the doctor![2]

The problem was not only the doctor's lack of anatomical knowledge, it was also primitive methods of aseptic technique and no effective way to prevent wound infections.

▶ *Charles Dickens came here to visit Poe's aunt, Mary Clemm, before she died at Church Home. Poe's work was widely read in Europe (not in America) and Dickens was anxious to have some first hand information on the character of Edgar Allan Poe.*

Church Hospital

Church Hospital and cross from the third fire of Old St. Paul's Church.

1 Let's begin this walk here at Baltimore Street and Broadway. In the center island there is a statue of Ferdinand Latrobe, grandson of B. H. Latrobe and five times mayor of Baltimore.

2 Up the hill and on your left is the Church Hospital and its Auxiliary Home for the Aged. This is Baltimore's oldest and most community oriented hospital. Since its inception, in 1857, the Church Home and Infirmary (its name until it changed in 1980) has always offered the optimum in patient care. It's nursing school graduates have never ceased to show the personal interest and concern which is essential to a patient's sense of well-being and to eventual recovery.

Note the building with the cupola. From 1836-1855 this building housed the Washington Medical College. It was here that Edgar Allan Poe died in October, 1849, and his body lay on view in the rotunda for two days.

The Church Home and Infirmary purchased the building in 1857 for $20,500. The cross on top of the cupola was originally on top of the third St. Paul's Episcopal Church which was destroyed by fire in 1855. Notice the nice, old iron-work entrances on either side of the driveway. Let's stroll up the driveway and look at the outside of the old building. It has some interesting ornamental brickwork.

3 As we leave the Church Hospital note the monument in the center island of Broadway. It was dedicated in 1865 to a man named Thomas Wildey. He founded the Independent Order of Odd Fellows at Fells Point in April, 1819. It was the first Odd Fellows Lodge in America.

4 On the corner of Broadway and Orleans is a modern branch of the Pratt Library. The sculpture in front is by Roger Majorwicz. Named "Paestum," it was placed here in January, 1971.

Johns Hopkins Hospital around 1920.

▶ *The hospital was built on the "pavillion system" with great stress on air and sunlight in order to prevent the transmission of disease. The wards spread out from the sides and rear of the administration building and were connected by corridors. In the middle was a garden. There was a complicated system of vents, flues and ducts to balance the circulation of air, but Baltimore had no sewage system. Excreta was discharged in privy pits and cesspools.[3]*

▶ *When Dr. William Osler agreed to take charge of managing the new hospital, D. C. Gilman, the president of the university assured him, "There is no difference between a hospital and a hotel." Everything was arranged in departments with responsible heads and a director over all.[4]*

▶ *Those of us who have grown up with the Hopkins as a part of our background never cease to enter this old building with a sense of respect which approaches reverence for the role Hopkins physicians and nurses have played in the development of clinical medicine and associated research. Osler referred to this aspect of medical care as "the quality of excellence."*

▶ *Johns Hopkins was a merchant, a banker, a bachelor (because the woman he loved rejected him), and a Quaker. He was a shrewd business man and*

5 The Johns Hopkins Hospital. The original Victorian building with its mosque-like dome is now dwarfed by the tall clinical buildings which have sprouted around it in the past two decades. Ignore them. Pause in front of the driveway and look at the three original buildings. On your left is the Marburg, once a male pay ward, then the posh spot where Ali Khan, Joe Dimaggio, and Cary Grant stayed. On your right is the Wilmer, once the female pay ward, now the famous eye clinic. In the center is the administration building. The hospital was designed by John Shaw Billings in 1877. It opened in May, 1889, with 220 beds. It now has 1,078 beds.

Billings was an army doctor who was commissioned by the original board of directors to search throughout the world for the best scientific and medically appropriate plan for a new hospital.

Let's mount the steps and enter the Administration Building. On the left hand wall is a life size portrait of Johns Hopkins painted from life by Thomas C. Corner.

Pratt Library

"Christus Consolator" in lobby of the Hopkins.

was hated by many of the people who knew him. He left $7,000,000 dollars to be divided equally to found a hospital and a university with an associated school of medicine. He donated the four block area of land on which the hospital stands and he specified that: "The indigent sick of this city and its environs shall be received into the hospital without charge...." It has been stated that certain people such as George Peabody encouraged him to bequeath his money in this manner. Johns Hopkins' estate was a mile north of here—in what is now known as Clifton Park.

▶ *It's difficult to know which important discoveries initiated at the Hopkins to list.*

    1. Dr. Hugh Young's work in early 1900 paved the way for all modern urology.

    2. Dramamine, the sulphanomides, and strepto- mycin, were developed. Vitamins A and D were discovered.

    3. Dr. Alfred Blalock and Dr. Helen Taussig with their work on "Blue Babies" in the mid 1940's paved the way for all future heart surgery.

    4. Psychiatry was recognized as a major discipline in a teaching hospital when the Phipps Clinic opened in 1913.

    5. The use of rubber gloves in surgery was origi- nated because Dr. William Halsted was in love with his chief operating room nurse and she had an allergy to the solutions they used to soak their hands. Dr. Halsted also did the first radical mastectomy and invented many types of sutures and instruments.

    6. Dr. Howard Kelly was the first to use radium for the treatment of growths and tumors.

    7. Dr. Osler was a masterful teacher of medicine. So was Dr. Welch—Popsy—as he was dearly called. He was also an authority on pathology.

▶ *The Johns Hopkins Hospital School for Nurses attracted intelligent young women from every State in the Union and even from Europe. It served as a model for other schools of nursing. Its graduates were in great demand. Some became national leaders in nursing, and one of its first graduates, Adelaide Nutting, originated the chair for teaching graduate*

The statue is the "Christus Consolator," copied from the original work of Bertel Thorwaldsen in Copenhagen and given to the Hopkins by an early trustee, William Spence. Mr. Spence said he wished to keep a religious spirit forever prevalent in the work of the hospital.

Look up—under the dome. The early medical residents lived on the three floors you see there. Students boarded with persons in the neighborhood. The professors lived in homes across town.

In the early 1950's hospitals finally stopped painting all their walls the color of urine and began to use lively tones. The blue you see matches the blue in the Cathedral in Copenhagen where the original "Christus" stands.

Now let's return to Broadway. Notice the high polish of the brass on the main door and the stair railing. When the hospital opened in 1889, and for many years thereafter, William Edward Thomas presided here. He wore a uniform and a blue and silver enamel pin which bore his name and the legend "J.H.H. from 1889 to Heaven." Do you see him?[5]

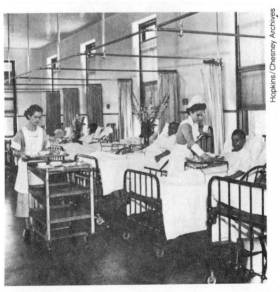

Hopkins/Chesney Archives

Student nurses on a ward at the Hopkins.

nurses at the master degree level at Columbia University. But the school curriculum was never permitted to be developed into a baccalaureate program and to become affiliated with the Hopkins University.

Hopkins/Chesney Archives

Isabel Hampton Robb, first Director of Nursing and Superintendent of the Hospital.

▶ In 1874 President Eliot of Harvard told the Hopkins Board of Trustees that coeducation was a wrong idea.... It could produce socially unequal and unacceptable marriages...it could threaten a woman's health...it would retard the pace of instruction to the detriment of the men...education of women should prepare them for a life which is fundamentally different from that of any man.[6]

The Hopkins Nurses' Alumnae Association never stopped battling for this privilege. The answer from the University was always the same: "Women are not permitted on campus in the daytime." There must have been some chauvinist enemies. The School of Nursing was forced to close its doors the very year that the University revised its policy and allowed Goucher College students (all female) to register for Hopkins University classes.

6 Hampton House is the red brick building directly across the street and was the second home for Hopkins nurses. The first was adjacent to the building we just left. No hospital can function without a staff of nurses to supplement the work of its doctors. Dr. Billings gave direction for this when he wrote to the first Hopkins board from Europe:

Miss Nightingale's views . . . and the Bellevue Hospital training school . . . hold that female nurses should be as far as possible, refined, educated women, fitted to move in good society, who should be throughly trained in everything pertaining to the management of the sick. . . . They should know as much as the surgeon about the dressing of wounds and as much as the physician about the meaning of symptoms — yet they must have no tendency to become medical women, or to set up their opinions in practice.[5]

The School of Nursing opened in October, 1889, five months after the hospital. Isabel Hampton was employed in the dual position of Superintendent of the hospital and Principal of the Training School. Eighty persons had applied, but she entered the interview room looking like an "animated Greek goddess" and got the job in 15 minutes.

Eighty-one years later, in June, 1970 the Johns Hopkins School of Nursing was phased out of existence. It was considered by the Hopkins Board of Trustees to be too expensive to be maintained. Hampton House became a building for new offices.

▶ When the hospital was new, its immediate neighbor was a pigeon house maintained by Arunah Abell, a founder of the Sunpaper. It contained 500-600 carrier pigeons which were trained to carry news between New York, Philadelphia, Baltimore and Washington. These were days prior to the telegraph and these pigeons were the predecessors of the Associated Press.

▶ The medical school opened two years after the hospital. It was the first to require that its students have a college degree, plus specific premedical courses. It was the first medical school to admit women. This was happenstance. The board ran out of money and was not able to complete the medical school buildings. Four Baltimore women: Miss Mary Garrett, Miss Mary Gwynn, Miss M. Carey Thomas, and Miss Elizabeth King formed a committee and raised $500,000 to be given to the school with the stipulation that women be part of the student body. This was women's lib in 1891! (Miss Thomas became Dean and later President of Bryn Mawr College.)

The medical school opened at a time when there was an international need for better medicine and high ideals to be espoused. The four great doctors created a unique chief resident system at the Hopkins, which trained men so thoroughly in their field of choice that when they left, they were qualified for the most sophisticated positions in medicine that the world had to offer.

▶ The four great doctors who came to Baltimore to organize the work at the Hopkins during its embryonic years brought with them the inspiration and the ingenuity which was the impetus for greatness. They were men of spirit, humanity and deep understanding of illness, disease and people.

▶ Under the astute direction of Dr. Adolf Meyer, the Phipps attracted international attention to its work. No hospital anywhere had yet admitted that psychiatry was a medically scientific discipline.

Hopkins/Chesney Archives

A graduating class, the first school of Nursing, in the Phipps garden.

7 On the northeast corner of Broadway at Monument Street is the John F. Kennedy Institute for Handicapped Children built in the late 1960's with monies donated by the Kennedy family and staffed with personnel from the Hopkins.

We'll walk east on Monument Street. You will pass the doorways which lead into the Johns Hopkins emergency room and to the various clinics. Notice the constant activity along the street. It's all associated with hospital business. Over 1,000 patients are seen in these clinics daily.

8 On your left is the Turner Auditorium, named for a former dean of the medical school. It contains a book store and usually has an interesting art exhibit in its lobby. Take a minute, if you like, and go see.

9 The Welsh Medical Library is the building on the northeast corner of Monument and Wolfe Streets. It has an interesting museum on the third floor and a wheel chair which belonged to Florence Nightingale. The famous portrait of the original four great Hopkins physicians: Halsted, Osler, Welch, and Kelly, painted in Europe by John Sargent hangs in its front room. The new buildings for the medical school may be seen along the northeast side of the same block.

▶ The Hopkins Nurses' Alumna Association never ceased to work toward academic recognition of their school's program. They subsidized its existence while it was still operated by Hospital Administration. They have had committees at work with members of the medical school faculty and with the University from 1900 until the present day. Finally, a school was opened in 1984 which offers a Bachelor of Science Degree. It is affiliated with the Hopkins University and there are plans afoot to create a Master level program in the next few years.

▶ There are several innovative housing redevelopment programs in this neighborhood.

Hopkins/Chesney Archives

A Goldseker slum.

▶ As late as 1960 this entire area was a hideous slum. Houses still had privies in the back. Most of it was owned by a man named Morris Goldseker. He was described as an absentee landlord. He made a fortune renting filth to the poor.

Then he wrote a will in which he created a foundation which would support charitable programs for the low income group he knew so well.

The will stipulated that the President of the Johns Hopkins University, the President of Morgan State University, and the President of the Associated Jewish Charities should constitute the selection committee which would make the funding decisions. Mr. Goldseker died in 1973. Since his death more than 150 grants have been made to programs in education, housing, human welfare, medicine and public health.[7]

The worst of the properties which he owned have been torn down.

10 Let's turn right and saunter down Wolfe Street. On your left, at 615 N. Wolfe Street is the School of Public Health and Hygiene which was given to the Hopkins in 1909 by John D. Rockefeller.

11 On your right is the new entrance to the hospital. Notice the fine old red brick building on the left side of the entrance. This was the Henry Phipps Psychiatric Clinic which opened in 1913.

Take a minute to visit and enjoy the fine marble lobby and the charming garden.

The iron bars have been removed from the windows and porches and the Phipps now contains the offices and classrooms for the **new** school of nursing which opened in 1984.

12 The old hospital laundry building is at the end of this block on the right. It is now used as a consolidated laundry service for five of the largest hospitals in the city. This idea originated here in the 1960's and has been universally copied.

13 On the west side of Wolfe Street beginning at 126 is another new and interesting project, built in 1983 with Government help.

"See," said the young builder, "They look just like early Baltimore. Stained glass in the transoms. Iron grill work on the outside steps. Just the way things used to be."

There are 89 units, costing $55,000-$65,000 and every one was sold before the builder had finished to young people working in the downtown area. A Federal Grant of $10,000 was available to each buyer and would not have to be paid back to the government if the buyer lived in the house for ten years. If he or she sells earlier, a portion of the loan must be returned. This was a plan to give young people a chance to buy their first home and to gain some equity.

We turn right at Baltimore Street to return to our starting point.

1. *Lumbee Indian houses*
2. *Bankard-Gunther House*
3. *Belmont Stables*
4. *Collington Avenue restoration*
5. *Converted city school*
6. *Blood Alley*
7. *Bonaparte houses*
8. *Baltimore Street plantings*
9. *Cannon in Patterson Park*
10. *Banner Neighborhoods, Inc.*
11. *Patterson Park Pagoda*
12. *Lombard Street rehabilitation*

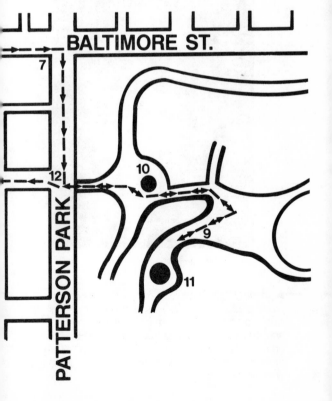

▶ The history of this area goes back to 1792 when land known as Kemp's Addition and Parker's Haven was sold at auction to William Patterson. At that time it was known as Hampstead Hill. It was 125 feet above sea level. 30 to 50 butchers settled here prior to the Civil War and went into business. It was close to the Philadelphia Road so livestock was easily obtained. The height was a natural defense against the smelly part of the business. There was actually a city ordinance passed in 1812 that outlawed the building of slaughter houses in the populated areas of the city.

These men became quite wealthy. They had stalls in every market in the city. By 1855 they were able to build large homes for themselves and smaller ones to rent to their employees.

Pratt Library

William Patterson.

▶ In early days, when the town of Baltimore was growing into a city, there was quite a problem with silt washing from this hill down into Washington, Wolfe, and Ann Streets, causing blockage. In 1808, a special commission ordered that Ann Street be rebuilt with a foot-wide concave which would channel the drainage downhill into the harbor.[1]

1 We're going to start at the corner of Baltimore Street at Washington and walk east.

The butchers performed all of the tasks associated with their trade on this hill. They killed the cattle, cured the beef and sold it in stalls or shops.

So when preservationists needed a name a few years ago they chose Butchers (without an apostrophe) Hill.

This 2000 block of Baltimore Street is where the Lumbee Indians now live. There was no special name for this neighborhood.

2 2101 E. Baltimore Street was built in 1864 by one of the wealthy butchers, Joseph J. Bankard. His family had started in business in 1840. By 1890 the butchers were dying out. There were twenty breweries in Baltimore and several of them were just north of here. This house was bought by George Gunther in 1890. He was the owner of one of the largest and most successful of the breweries in East Baltimore.

DRINK

White and Gold

THE

GEO. GÜNTHER, JR.

BREWING COMPANY

Toone and Third Streets

BALTIMORE, MARYLAND

3 2115-2117 E. Baltimore Street were opened as the Belmont Stables in 1892. This was a place where a personal horse could be boarded or a horse and buggy could be rented.

▶ *Butchers Hill is another neighborhood which went down hill after World War II. In the latter part of the 1970's the Southeast Community Organization created the Southeast Landbank. They got a $568,000 loan from the Ford Foundation and bought about 100 houses from absentee landlords. They then sold the properties to homeowners who were required to abide by restrictions which limited the number of units in each house and determined that the buildings should be restored as dwelling units instead of the places of business which many had become.[2]*

Building and Loan Associations were willing to make generous loans for rehab purposes. The cost per house was $7,000 - $17,000. Most of the houses are now close to their original appearance both inside and out.

T. Chandlee

Gunther/Bankert House.

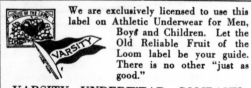

4 When you reach Collington Avenue you might enjoy turning left and walking one block north. 100-114 Collington have been restored. They began life as homes for humble working class people. They have been up-graded to stylish homes for middle class working people and young professionals.

5 A block west of Collington, at Chester Street and Fayette, is a large city school which has recently been converted into nice apartments.

6 We'll walk back down Collington to Baltimore Street. Notice Lamley Street as you cross it. It was once named Blood Alley because most of the cattle were slaughtered along here. The rains would wash the blood down the hill.

Peale Museum

Patterson Park Avenue and Baltimore Street in 1932.

7 Notice the prim stateliness of the houses along the 2200 block of Baltimore Street. Mencken referred to them as the old placid rows. The group on the southwest corner of Baltimore Street and Patterson Park Avenue were built in 1884 by Charles Joseph Bonaparte, Betsy Patterson's grandchild, and Secretary of the Navy under Theodore Roosevelt.

Banner Neighborhoods

New resident, Charles Kerrow improves his Butchers Hill block.

▶ *William Patterson gave this land to the city in 1827 but it was not made a public park until 1853. The city has added to the original acreage through the years.*

▶ *Neither Britain nor America wanted another war. The one in 1812-1814 occurred because each was badgering the other. In 1803 there was an incident on this hill which proved this. An American ship, the Sophia, had been held up at sea by the British and forced to pay a tax on the 720 gallons of Holland gin in her hole. When the ship anchored in the port of Baltimore this news circulated. A town meeting was held. The townspeople were so angry that more than 1,600 people marched to Hampstead Hill where the 720 gallons of gin was burned while a band played "Yankee Doodle."*[3]

▶ *In the summertime the residents of Fells Point frequently camped here in order to avoid typhoid and yellow fever.*

Betsy Patterson and Jerome Bonaparte meet.

8 The planting in front of various houses was done by residents. It is illegal to disturb historic property. When the city was asked if portions of the sidewalk could be removed for this purpose the answer was. "Do it, but don't tell us about it."

9 Baltimore Street dead-ends at Patterson Park Avenue. Just opposite is Patterson Park, the first park in Baltimore. Enter through the elaborate cement gates and stroll over to the knoll at the right. The cannons you see are the ones which were frantically placed here on a Sunday afternoon in 1814.

They were a portion of the fortification which saved Baltimore from falling into the hands of the British in the Battle of North Point.

Patterson Park Fountain circa 1920.

Pratt Library

Patterson Park Observatory.

▶ *We were able to obtain an old family recipe for scrubbing white marble steps from Maureen Abbott.*
WHITE MARBLE STEPS
  1. *1 quart of muratic acid. Mix with water as directed on the bottle.*
  2. *Use rubber gloves, a scrub brush and apply the acid to the steps.*
  3. *Rinse with water.*
  4. *Re-scrub with Comet which has been liberally sprinkled on the steps. Let the foam sit for five minutes before rinsing. This seals the pores.*

▶ *This was Maureen's Irish mother's recipe. "Let ice drip off the steps in the winter," says Maureen. "Don't* **never** *try to chip it off with an ice pick. This would leave lasting scars and the steps would never polish up bright again."*

10 The charming house to the left of the gate is the caretaker's cottage, built about 1865. It has been restored by volunteers and houses Banner Neighborhoods. This is a community organization with a variety of programs. Do stop in. They love to show off their headquarters.

11 The Patterson Observatory, known as the Pagada, was designed by Charles H. Latrobe and placed here in 1891.[4]

12 When you are ready to leave the park, walk down Lombard Street. This is the most marvelous view we know. Look down the hill and see the skyline of the city. At sunset this view is breathtaking. The houses on both sides of the street are in various stages of rehabilitation.

Peek to the left as you reach a cross street. Each opening presents a different view of the harbor. Much of it is being transformed by various sorts of dwelling units. Real estate values are sky rocketing. An industrial area is becoming a residential one. Our ancestors would shudder . . . we think.

When you reach Washington Street turn right. A block away is Baltimore Street where we began.

NOTES South Baltimore

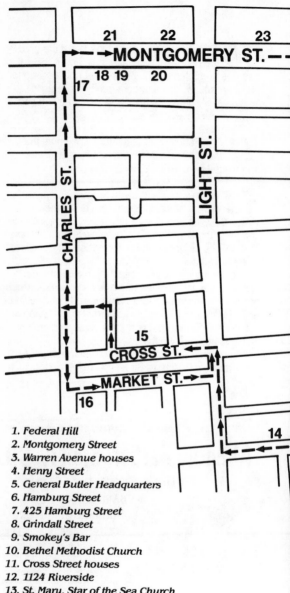

21 22 23

→ MONTGOMERY ST. — —

18 19 20

17

CHARLES ST.

LIGHT ST.

15

CROSS ST. ←

← MARKET ST. →

16

14

1. Federal Hill
2. Montgomery Street
3. Warren Avenue houses
4. Henry Street
5. General Butler Headquarters
6. Hamburg Street
7. 425 Hamburg Street
8. Grindall Street
9. Smokey's Bar
10. Bethel Methodist Church
11. Cross Street houses
12. 1124 Riverside
13. St. Mary, Star of the Sea Church
14. Holy Cross Church
15. Cross Street Market
16. Muhly's Bakery
17. South Charles Street restored houses

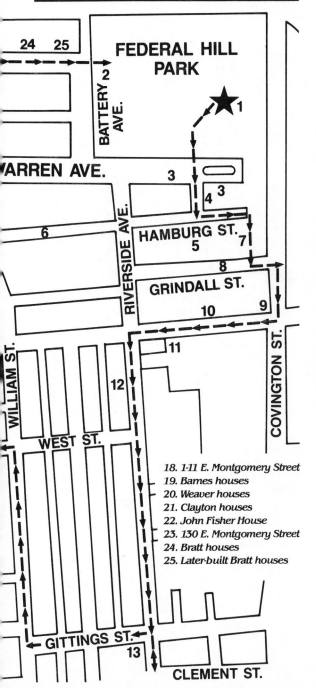

FEDERAL HILL PARK

BATTERY AVE.

24 25

WARREN AVE.

RIVERSIDE AVE.

6

3

3

4

HAMBURG ST.
5

7

8

GRINDALL ST.

10 9

11

12

COVINGTON ST.

WILLIAM ST.

WEST ST.

18. 1-11 E. Montgomery Street
19. Barnes houses
20. Weaver houses
21. Clayton houses
22. John Fisher House
23. 130 E. Montgomery Street
24. Bratt houses
25. Later-built Bratt houses

GITTINGS ST.

13

CLEMENT ST.

123

▶ In April, 1788, the Maryland Senate adopted the Federal Constitution. Federal Hill was named to honor that event and 3,000 Baltimoreans attended a party here to celebrate the occasion.

▶ In 1789, Captain David Porter built an observation tower in order to run up an owner's flag when one of his ships was spotted coming up the Bay. Three hundred early merchants subscribed to this service.

Federal Hill in 1861.

▶ For a while, a ferry connected the Hill to Jonestown — just across the harbor. Then in 1859, Dr. Thomas Buckler wanted to shovel the Hill into the Harbor. Dr. Buckler was a pioneer in the fight to purify sewage disposal in order to stop the spread of contagious disease. He was quite outspoken: "Baltimore needs to rid itself of that pampered and cherished puddle it calls a harbor."[1] His strongest opponents were the group of merchants on Light Street whose property was threatened. Among these were Henry Walters, Johns Hopkins and Enoch Pratt. Buckler referred to them as the "House of Piers." He had plans drawn to illustrate his point. If Federal Hill was levelled the soil could be used in part to fill in the basin and the stagnant water, which was a breeding place for vermin, rodents and bacteria, could be syphoned away. His engineer's plans for this were snitched from the desks of city councilmen just minutes before they met to consider the issue.[2] Thus was Dr. Buckler defeated.

▶ In 1861 a garrison of Union Troops was camped here.

1 Federal Hill. We'll begin our tour with a walk around the perimeter of the hill. The view of the port is a panoramic one and it's easy to see the "Renaissance" skyline and the more prosaic shipping, warehouse and loading sections. The two monuments were moved here from other places.

The Hill and its immediate environs are riddled with underground passageways. There have always been rumors that they lead to Fort McHenry — two miles away. This is not true. Iron ore, clay and sand were mined for a while from veins in sections of the Hill. The honeycombs were the result.

Pratt Library

Federal Hill during the Civil War.

▶ Baltimore loyalties during the War between the States were literally split in two. Many of the spies and blockade runners were women. The Monument Street girls and the Secesh Babies were two groups of socially prominent and attractive women who, against *all* regulations, wore the red and white colors of the South and baited and heckled the Union men based on Federal Hill.

▶ In the 1960's the State Roads Administration had plans to build an extension of I-70 through here. The Society for the Preservation of Federal Hill, and Fell's Point was formed in 1967. It brought a citizen's suit against the construction of this highway and also of I-83 which would cut through Fell's Point. The fight lasted 9 years. The highways were built elsewhere.

▶ The Port of Baltimore is 45 miles of inland water-way. It is not as visible as other ports such as New York where the land is flat and the entrance to the Harbor is a wide expanse of water. Here the land is hilly and uneven. There used to be freighters in the docks directly below you. Now the area is being developed for housing. A highrise condominium is going up. It is not as high as was originally planned though. The new residents of this section went to war and opposed it so a compromise was made.

Pratt Library

Fort Federal Hill.

2 Montgomery Street can be seen *in toto* from the western side of the hill. Let's look down on it for a minute. In 1960 this was a blighted area. Two and three families were crowded into each small house. Heat came only from a pot belly stove in the living room. So did food. There was a pot of beans on top of this stove and children used a wooden spoon to eat these beans for three meals a day — plus in between snacks. In 1967 these families were relocated. In 1978, the city sold the houses to private persons for prices ranging from $4,000 to $7,000 with the stipulation that they be restored. Today these houses sell for $150,000 and up. There were not enough to go around so developers began to look southward. We are about to see what has happened. Let's leave the Hill by the Warren Avenue exit.

3 345-335 Warren Avenue are examples of the kind of row house built in Baltimore from 1900-1912. 403-413 were built for shipowners around 1885.

4 Henry Street to Hamburg is paved with cobblestone and is an original early Baltimore roadway.

T. Chandlee

Hughes Street House where General Butler stood on the balcony in the Civil War and watched as Southern sympathizers were shot in the back yard.

▶ *Gittings was a banker who dabbled with real estate investments. These houses were built for the working class. Each contains two rooms 11x12 feet deep on the first floor with a narrow kitchen. There are two equal size rooms on the second floor and a single room under the dormer. Every house had a small back yard with an outdoor privy.*

▶ *Struever Brothers and Eccles had a plan for a quick renovation of homes in combination with commercial rehabilitation. They were able to persuade the Baltimore Federal Savings and Loan Association to lend them money so that they could begin work on the houses we just saw on Grindall Street. They worked quickly. They could and did completely renovate a small house in three months time.*

They wanted to attract more monied people back into the city, but they did not wish to displace families who had lived here for generations. Through their special banking connections they provided financing plans for tenants in south Baltimore who wished to purchase and to improve the houses which they occupied.

▶ *In 1846 Captain Samuel Kramer established a church on the wrecked hull of a ship named the William Penn. It was anchored in the water opposite the McCormick plant until 1853 when it was considered to*

5 337 Hamburg Street was built about 1810 and is the oldest house in the block. When Union troops were stationed on Federal Hill their General, Benjamin Butler, used this house as his headquarters. Rebel spies were held prisoner in the basement, and General Butler stood on the second story porch to watch their executions in the yard below.

6 Hamburg Street. The majority of these houses were built by a man named John Gittings between 1835-1845. They sold for $700-$900.[3] It's easy to spot those which have been bought and rehabilitated. Let's turn left when you are ready.

7 425 Hamburg Street is a perennial favorite for people who visit the Hill. It was built about 1830 and was formerly two houses. Notice the two side porches and the dogwood tree. And what a view of the water!

8 Grindall Street, we love this name, it sounds so Dickensonian. Take a quick look at the houses on the right at the crest of the hill. They were among the first to be restored as a part of an interesting plan for renovation which was developed in 1975 by the young group named Struever Brothers and Eccles. Each of the three partners was only in his twenties. Within one year they remodeled and sold twelve of the houses on Grindall Street. In 1977 they won the House of the Year Award given by the Maryland Improvement Contractor's Association for urban renewal remodeling.

9 We'll walk down Covington one block to Cross Street.
   Smokey's Bar, at the corner of Covington and Cross Streets, is now gone. It was a sailor's bar — opened in the 1800's and closed within the past three years.

10 Three doors down was the Sailor's Union Bethel Methodist Church built in 1873. It was called The Ship Church, and sailors still drop in for Sunday Services. The exterior of the building was restored in 1976 by Struever Brothers and Eccles in time for the 130th anniversary celebration.

be unsafe. The congregation was wayward sailors and some Baltimoreans who were interested in them.

When the William Penn was condemned they moved from place to place until they raised enough money to buy this building and convert it into a place to worship.

▶ The houses on Cross Street were built for James J. Morgan between 1885-1895. They were sold for $1,200-$1,400 to mariners, grocers, carpenters, butchers, shoemakers and laborers.[4] By this time building and loan associations had been organized to assist special ethnic group members to become homeowners.

▶ The majority of the people who settled in this area were Irish and German. They built their own churches. In the evening, after work, they came with picks and shovels to dig the foundations and then hired brick-layers, carpenters, etc. to erect the buildings. Most of the inside furnishings came from Europe.

▶ Payment for the building was the responsiblity of the Pastor. Fairs, carnivals, strawberry festivals and harvest homes had paid the debt for St. Mary Star of the Sea by 1900. Twelve years later, in 1912, they went in debt again, this time to build a school which cost $75,000.

▶ Jealousy was intense among the ethnic groups which came to settle in America. Each was vying for blue collar jobs in a limited market and for status in the community. The Irish were especially close-knit and wanted no one but their own inside their churches. The Germans were deathly afraid that they would lose their faith if they lost their language. The Mass was internationally celebrated in Latin, but the celebrants were required to speak the German lan-guage in every other instance.

11 Many of these houses on Cross Street were *rehabbed* by the Struever Brothers and Eccles and sold to professional people. Notice how carefully the front facades have been restored in order to preserve the original character of the street. Inside, they are quite modern with new kitchens, solar heat and air conditioning.

Let's turn left at Riverside Avenue and pause for a minute to see the spire of St. Mary, Star of the Sea. In the center of the cross, on top of the steeple, is a light which has been a beacon to seamen since 1871.

12 1124 Riverside was originally two houses, the type known as "half houses" or "alley houses" which were one room deep. The houses were built in 1830-1840 to be rented to free slaves and immigrants who were struggling to find a place for themselves in the labor market.

Notice the archways between some of the houses on the left. They led to livery stables behind these houses.

13 St. Mary, Star of the Sea was built by the Irish residents of this area in 1871. This was a time when the Catholic Church in America was obliged to create new parishes and new orders of priests and teaching nuns in order to cope with ethnic differences.

In 1960, the Vatican decided to "modernize" all Catholic Churches and to simplify the appearance of the altar. This decision created fury among certain parishes. This was one of them. Many of the most beautiful and valuable treasures of this Church were wantonly destroyed by young reactionaries, causing a deep and unforgivable distress to older members of the congregation.

The parish house is at 1419 Riverside Avenue. Phone 685-2255 to see inside.

▶ *This particular parish was organized in 1859 by a German group of the Catholic Church who were known as the Redemptorists, an international colony of mission societies with bases in Belgium and Austria. They were an intellectually active group who were interested in teaching and in community organization, so much so that they spread out away from Baltimore and followed German immigrants into railroad and mining towns and even established new settlements. They were so meticulously organized that many people think they were responsible for the first building and loan organizations in Baltimore.*[5]

Pratt Library

Federal Hill Observatory.

▶ *Baltimore has always been a market town. Since its conception, the life forces of every neighborhood in this city have orbited around its market. The original wooden buildings for this market burned in 1951. In its current form, the market is an example of the commercial revitalization which was inspired by Struever Brothers and Eccles. Patapsco Street, on the north side of the market, contains several small shops located in old houses. The Struevers cut an alley way from Patapsco to Charles Street. Wander through.*

14 We'll walk north on William Street to West Street and then left. The Holy Cross Church was begun in 1858 and finished in 1885. It has been refurbished and is bubbling with a vitality which was missing in the 1960's and '70s. The lovely stained glass windows have been repaired, the church has been cleaned, and the interior paint is now the vibrant coloring which existed in the original building.

Entrance is gained by phoning 742-8498.

Now let's stroll right down West Street to Light, turn right and walk to Cross Street Market.

15 Cross Street Market was founded in January, 1846. Nearly all of the vendors are descended from original South Baltimore families. Most of them are on a first name basis with their customers. The raw bar is considered by many to be the best in the city. There are some interesting European foods. Let's stop in. Look for freshly ground coconut. It's a specialty here.

16 1115 S. Charles Street is the bakery which was founded by Eberhardt Muhly in 1852 in a small house just below Federal Hill. Women in the area would mix their dough and would pay Mr. Muhly two cents a loaf to bake their bread in his oven with his own. His bread was good, but it cost five cents a loaf. The sixth generation of Muhlys now run the business.

T. Chandlee

Muhly's Bakery.

▶ *Montgomery is the most charming and hence the most popular of the streets in the Federal Hill restoration. The houses were bought at prices ranging from $4,000-$10,000 from the city and from private owners. There were no standards to control the restoration. Most people just naturally tended to want them to assume their original outside appearance. Such thinking was encouraged by the Commission for Historical and Architectural Preservation. This is a city sponsored organization, which tries very hard to uphold the proper preservationist controls on historic properties. Unhappily, because it is under city jurisdiction, politicians can and often do intervene to contradict its decisions.*

▶ *When the new residents discovered that cobblestones were underneath the tar which topped Montgomery Street, they got out picks and shovels and broke up the tar in the 100 block. City officials asked what they could do to help. They could, of course, have had the tar removed from the entire area. They didn't, but they sent a truck to haul the broken tar away, which was of some help.*

▶ *Fisher brought the plans for this house with him when he came here from Philadelphia. It is the only house of its size in this section of Federal Hill.[6] The original doorway was removed and is on permanent display at the Baltimore Museum of Art. This was the standard middle class house of the period.*

▶ *It is fortunate that such early Baltimore housing has remained. In 1981, Mary Ellen Hayward did a detailed report on it for the Henry Francis du Pont Winterthur Museum. We have used information from this report to describe houses on Montgomery Street.*

17 Now we'll walk north on Charles Street to Montgomery Street and turn right.

18 Numbers 1-11 E. Montgomery Street were built between 1800 and 1810 by people who rented lots from a man named David Williamson. These homes are only one room deep. The original kitchens were located in a narrow back buildings, which were attached to the homes only by roofs.[8]

19 Numbers 9 and 11 are joint homes built by a carter named Ford Barnes in 1801. He lived in #9 and rented #11.

20 Number 1 and number 3 were built by a bricklayer named Lewis Weaver in 1801. He sold them both two years later to a blacksmith.

21 2-12 E. Montgomery Street are described as two story plus attic Greek revival style. They were built in 1848 by Samuel Clayton.[9]

22 Number 36 is the first brick house to have been built on Federal Hill. The builder was John Fisher, a carpenter from Philadelphia, who operated an inn and boarding house here when the house was completed in 1795.[10]

23 130 E. Montgomery Street is a two story frame house built about 1796 by John Murray. It is an example of the style of house that was built in Baltimore Town and Fells Point until 1799 when a fire law mandated brick houses. This one was built by a boatman named Matthew Murray.[11]

24 206 and 208 E. Montgomery Street were built about 1853 by Samuel Bratt.

25 226-240 E. Montgomery Street were built in 1870-1871 by Samuel Bratt. Note the ways in which the styles altered mildly with the years. Most of them were built to be rented. If they were sold, the price was about $1,000.[12]

NOTES South Baltimore

1. *Lawrence Street*
2. *Francis Scott Key School*
3. *Our Lady of Counsel Church*
4. *Latrobe Park*
5. *B&O Railroad Yards*
6. *Locust Point Marine Terminal*
7. *Fort McHenry*
8. *Baltimore Museum of Industry*
9. *Rallo's Restaurant*

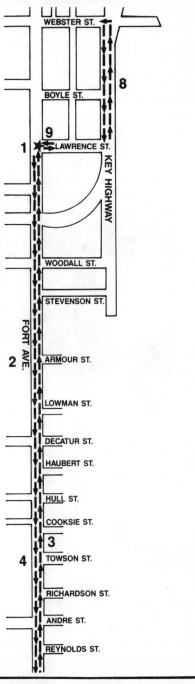

WEBSTER ST.

BOYLE ST.

8

KEY HIGHWAY

9

1 LAWRENCE ST.

WOODALL ST.

STEVENSON ST.

FORT AVE.

2 ARMOUR ST.

LOWMAN ST.

DECATUR ST.

HAUBERT ST.

HULL ST.

COOKSIE ST.

3

4 TOWSON ST.

RICHARDSON ST.

ANDRE ST.

REYNOLDS ST.

5 RAILROAD YARDS   **TO FORT McHENRY**
6   7

▶ This is a wonderful example of a way in which a nice old building can be recycled and reused. The center offers free art classes to talented children and low rent work space to eligible Baltimore artists. There are frequent gallery exhibits, lectures and workshops.

Peale Museum

Immigrants aboard steamer at the B&O's Railroad's Locust Point immigration facility, in 1904.

▶ Locust Point ranked second only to Ellis Island as large numbers of immigrants swarmed into America. They were essentially humble people from Germany, Ireland, Poland, Russia, Hungary and Czechoslovakia looking for a better life. They took any job they could get. None of them could read the language, or write it. Few of them could speak it. Men took jobs loading ship's holds, or pushing coal cars for the railroad. The women learned to pack in the canneries. Families lived in a rented room.

▶ As these people adjusted to the new life they developed a common canon: to be an American was to own your own home. It became an obsession. Both men and women began to accumulate overtime pay. The day they turned twelve, children were taken out of

An optional beginning for this tour is at 1427 Light Street. This is an early Baltimore Primary School Building, built in 1880. In 1979, it became a center for art and made its purpose technical assistance to working artists and promotion of greater public understanding and appreciation for contemporary visual art of every sort.

Gallery hours are: Tuesday-Saturday 11 am-4 pm. Phone: 396-4641

1 We'll start our walk at Lawrence Street and Fort Avenue. This is the northern boundary for Locust Point. To the people who live here anyone who comes from west of the railroad tracks which line the center of Lawrence Street is:

"Up from the Hill."

"An outsider."

"Lucky if we let him in."

No one can remember how the rivalry started. It's not too serious any more, but people who live in the Federal Hill area say they are from South Baltimore. People who live in Locust Point say they live in Locust Point, near Baltimore.

Peale Museum

Money changing booth at the B&O Railroad's Locust Point immigration facility in 1904.

school and put into factories to work. By 1900 the average stevedore was earning $500 a year.[1]

Builders began to put up blocks and blocks of row houses two stories high with "all the new conveniences" such as hot air furnaces, electric wiring, complete indoor plumbing and full basements. Families invested their savings in building and loan associations so that plans for mortgage payments could be developed. With every member of the family working there was eventually enough money to make a down payment on the house.[3]

Then a second canon evolved: to be clean because only the poor were dirty. Scrubbing became a ritual. Steps, windows, curtains, floors, children and on Saturday night, husbands. Notice the prim tidiness of each house as you pass by. They seldom go on the market. They are willed to sons or daughters, nieces or nephews, cousin to cousin.

T. Chandlee

The foot of Hull Street where Father Gibbons landed.

▶ In 1862, Father Gibbons was also the pastor for Saint Bridget's in Canton, on the opposite side of the harbor. This was no problem for him. He simply rowed across the harbor and docked his boat at the foot of Hull Street. He heard confession at Our Lady of Good Counsel on Sunday, preached on Sunday, visited the sick, and rowed back to Canton in time for mass. On each side of the harbor his parishioners were humble laborers who were consistently used by those with better jobs in management. The intense patriotism of Father Gibbons and his acute interest in the immigrant population of his congregations were very strong forces in the acculturation of this section of Baltimore.[4]

2 Francis Scott Key School. Schooling for children has been a major concern since the evolution of Locust Point. In 1851, one of the new settlers had a school in her living room. In 1881, the City Council allocated $10,000 for a coed school to be built at the corner of Clement and Hull Streets. It was named the Francis Scott Key School and contained eight elementary classrooms. In 1921, P.S. #76, the new Francis Scott Key School, was opened and represented the epitome of modernity. It was among the first public schools in the city to contain flush toilets, showers, a lunchroom, an auditorium, a kindergarten, a gymnasium and drinking fountains.[2]

For the children in Locust Point it served to finalize the Americanization of their settlement. English **had** to be spoken. Vaccinations **had** to be given. Contagious diseases **had** to be reported. Attendance was compulsory.

3 Our Lady of Good Counsel Church was completed in 1889 at great expense to its congregation. The Parish was established in 1859 and known as the Mission of St. Laurence O'Toole. Its first pastor was the Reverend James Gibbons who was to become Cardinal Gibbons and destined to play an international role in the primary definition of labor-management relationships. His unique concern was born as he worked among these first parishoners. Entrance to the church is through the Parish Office at 1532 E. Fort Avenue. Special visits may be arranged by phoning 752-0205.

Pratt Library

Cardinal Gibbons in 1913.

▶ The stevedore/shoreman jobs which the men on the Point have held for several generations are hard, dangerous and require a great deal of skill. They are replaced by word of mouth. There is also a dialect of phrases, puns and profanities which is specific to this profession. Listen for it.

▶ Notice the enormous cranes along the shoreline opposite the Park. To Locust Point residents they represent "containerization" which came to be about 20 years ago when machines replaced stevedores in loading boxes and crates onto ships.

▶ Few Baltimoreans know that national industries exist in Locust Point. The Domino Sugar Company, The Coca-Cola Company, and Proctor and Gamble have major plants here. The city of Baltimore has sold the ends of ten narrow streets to Proctor and Gamble and to Indiana Grain for $1.00 a street. This gives each of the two companies the right to build along the water's edge. They probably pay rent or right of way to the city annually.

German Evangelical Church at foot of Decatur Street.

4 Latrobe Park is a popular place in the neighborhood for recreation. There is an excellent local soccer team. Let's sit on a bench for a moment. The place was named Locust Point to commemorate the trees which grow here.

There are several ways for you to explore Locust Point. The best is to wander down some side streets. At the foot of Hull Street is a narrow two board pier. Imagine Father Gibbons' row boat tied to its end.

At the foot of Andre Street is a fine view of the grain elevator which is in use by the Indiana Grain Company.

At the foot of Decatur Street is an interesting German Church, built in 1886 and still a very active force in the community. "A thorn in the side of Proctor and Gamble" says one member of the congregation, "They want our land and we won't budge."

This little intrigue is a marvelous example of the pride and tenacity of Locust Point citizens. "We don't even get a bar of soap from them," one of the residents said. "But they are planting some trees along the road to hide the buildings. . . .The Coca-Cola Company has given uniforms to the little league baseball team."

Next door to the church is a building known as the Immigrant House. This is where incoming foreigners stayed for 10 cents a night until they found a job or were united with their sponsor. It is now used for Sunday School classes and work space for the Women of the Christ Church.

Every house you see along the way is owned by someone who is related to someone else on Locust Point.

Let's resume our walk southward.

▶ *The great railroad empires began to be built the day the Civil War ended in 1865. The Pennsylvania was a dangerous rival to the Baltimore and Ohio. B&O President, John Garrett took the offensive and he built big docks, warehouses and grain elevators here in Locust Point. The businessmen of Baltimore said the B&O had three periods of history: Before Garrett, Garrett and after Garrett.[5]*

B&O Archives

Aerial view of the B&O Railroad yards at Locust Point in 1936.

▶ *Francis Scott Key was a young lawyer who had gone aboard an English ship to seek the release of a friend who had been taken prisoner. He was forced to stay on the ship while it moved up the river and anchored. He was in a perfect spot to see Mary Pickersgill's big flag floating over the Fort. Night came. He began to watch for the flag every time there was a flash of light from bombs and rockets. In the morning, when it was still there, he scribbled his poem on an envelope and stuck it in his pocket. Later, friends in the city liked the verses so much that they had them printed. "The Star Spangled Banner" was sung at the Holliday Street Theater.*

5 The railroad yards. As we cross Reynolds Street you should begin to get a feel for the influence the railroad had in the growth and development of shipping industries into Locust Point. Look on both sides of the bridge.

The warehouse on the left was used to store tobacco.

6 The Locust Point Marine Terminal fits around the approach to Fort McHenry like a glove. It is a complex of piers and has had a variety of owners since the 1800s. Visitors are not welcome.

Pratt Library

Battle of Fort McHenry.

7 Fort McHenry was one of several sea coast fortifications which were built in America between 1794 and 1808. It was named for James McHenry of Maryland, who was Secretary to George Washington during the Revolution, and Secretary of War from 1796-1800.

During the Civil War the Fort was used as a prison for Baltimoreans with southern sympathies.

During World War I an Army Hospital was based here.

The Fort has been under the direction of the National Park Service since 1933. It is now a National Shrine.

In September, 1814, 16 English ships anchored off of North Point. Someone in England had decided that Baltimore was "a nest of privateers and needed to be tamed."[6] On September 11, 1814 Baltimoreans were leaving their churches after the 11 am service when they heard that the British ships were coming up the

Pratt Library

Fort McHenry.

Bay. They rushed to fortify the city as best they could. The British forces marched up North Point on September 12. Their General was killed by sharpshooters, but there was a bitter fight which lasted all day. There were heavy losses. The Baltimore troops apparently made the British think that their numbers were greater than they actually were. The enemy retreated. The next day, at 2 am, they began to bomb Fort McHenry from the water. The soldiers at the Fort laid low until the British drew close enough to be within range. Then they fired with vengence . . . and won.

The visitor center and Fort is open from 8:15 am-7:45 pm. Admission fee.

You may wish to take the bus back to Lawrence Street. There is one more visit we want you to have.

8 Walk east on Lawrence Avenue and left on Key Highway to 1415. This is the Museum of Industry. The building was once an oyster cannery. It contains a variety of displays such as the machinery and implements used in industries which shaped the city's destiny. Our favorite is the red Davidson Transfer vehicle. How much of your furniture would fit into it?

The Museum is open Saturday: 10 am-5 pm: Sunday: 12 noon-5 pm. Weekdays by appointment.

9 At 838 Fort Avenue is Rallo's. This is a small family owned restaurant where the food is excellent and inexpensive. Why not stop in for a bite and reflect on your visit to Locust Point.

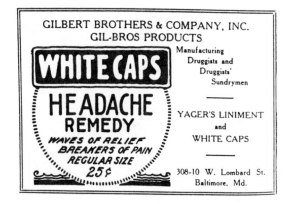

1. Sharp and Barre Streets
2. Otterbein houses
3. 511/523 Sharp Street
4. 529 Sharp Street
5. 613-626 Sharp Street
6. Church of the Lord Jesus Christ
7. Federal Reserve Bank
8. 811 Sharp Street
9. Greenspace
10. York Alley
11. 123/118 Lee Street
12. Convent/Berry House
13. 132 W. Lee/Captain Paulson House
14. Hanover Street
15. Welcome Alley
16. Barre Street

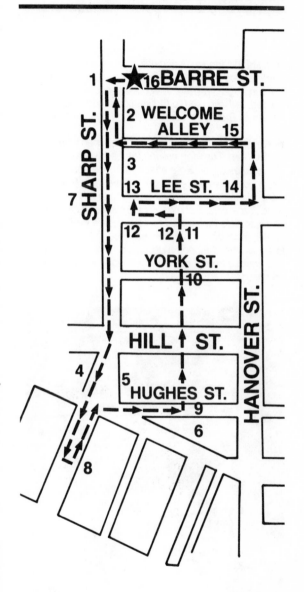

▶ All of this land was originally part of "Lund's Lott," a tract deeded to John Eager Howard, Jr., the grandson of John Eager Howard. In 1766, this section was sub-divided and annexed to the section around the harbor known as Baltimore Town. Building began in 1780.

▶ Row housing was expedient to the men who settled here. The land around the harbor was craggy and houses which were attached to one another could be built in groups of six, eight or ten. There were few trained architects and no schools so ambitious carpenters and masons appropriated the title and went into business. They used illustrated pattern books, most of which were published in New England, to show what they could do. Customers could pick and choose from a modest variety of housing styles and architectural details.

Pratt Library

A lunchroom in 1932.

1 We start at the corner of Sharp and Barre Streets and head south. Homesteading of early housing had begun in Wilmington and Philadelphia prior to Baltimore. There were 108 single family houses available here to be bought for $1.00. 800 people applied. Winners were selected by lottery.

The houses on your left were shells. The walls still stood, but many roofs and ceilings had collapsed. There were outhouses in the back. Homesteaders had the privilege of borrowing money from the city at less then market interest rate, but each one had to prove his or her ability to fund the work which had to be done and each had to agree to move into the house to live six months after the rehabilitation work had begun.

Note the hardware on these houses. Doorknobs, house numbers, mail slots, entry lights, and door knockers also had to meet the standards of the experts. You have probably noticed that the street lights are an eighteenth century design.

"Guidelines for Exterior Restoration" published by the Department of Housing and Community Development stated that all plans had to be approved by this organization AND the outside of every house had to look as it did when it was originally constructed about 1790-1820. Builders of the larger houses had been able to afford a hard brick. Smaller houses had been made from more porous brick. For a while there was a salvage depot on Pratt Street—a treasure house for preservationists—full of old doors, marble steps, fireplaces, lintels, foot scrapers, windows, and all sorts of bricks. This was loot from other old houses in the city which had been destroyed for one reason or another.

The shutters are identical to those used in 1790. Their purpose then was security not shade.
Notice the black iron clasps beneath them. These are shutter dogs.

Windows could not be taken out or changed in any way. Neither could they be blocked with air conditioners or storm windows. These amenities could be attached to the back of the house where they did not detract. The same was true of television aerials. They had to be put in back of the front roof line.

▶ Because everyone was associated with the harbor in some way, rich and poor lived side by side in early Baltimore. That is why the houses you now see are so diverse in size and shape and why the roof lines are so wonderfully irregular.

The population changed with the years. In 1860 this section was almost exclusively inhabited by German immigrants. By 1910 the population was Jewish and Italian, many of whom had small businesses in their homes.

In 1971 this area was described to me as the city's worst slum. There was nothing here but rats and a few immobilized, impoverished blacks. The houses were condemned. They were vacated, boarded against occupancy by vagrants and scheduled to be torn down.

▶ The Sharp Street area is synonymous with the evolution of black history in Maryland.

Because of its location, just a few miles north of Washington, D.C., Baltimore has always been seen as a haven, first for runaway slaves, then for freed slaves and itinerant blacks, especially those from Georgia and the Carolinas. In 1789, Elisha Tyson, a Quaker and local merchant who lived in this area, formed the Maryland Society for the Abolition of Slavery. Membership consisted of "all the most respectable class in Baltimore."[1] In 1796 this Society won a legislative fight to grant owners the right to free their slaves and in 1797, at 112-116 Sharp Street the Society opened a school known as The Baltimore Black Academy. Tyson's belief was that slavery was amoral. The purpose of his Society was to "protect the colored population of this State in the enjoyment of their legal privileges."[2]

2 The houses with pitched roofs are known as "Federal-style." Notice that they are quite plain and vary from two story with a dormer under the roof to a full three story. This type of house was put up in Baltimore at the end of the seventeenth century.

The three story houses with flat roofs and etched designed cornice and more elaborate doorways are "Greek-revival," a style which came to Baltimore about 1820.

3 511 & 523 Sharp Street are known as "store-fronts" which means that someone once had a store in the ground floor of his house. Rehabilitators were allowed to enclose the front in order to make an attractive residence.

4 529 & 531 Sharp Street was once the Tepper Hotel. In the 1940s it was known as the nicest whorehouse in town.

Notice that 603 & 605, and 609 & 611 are twin houses. It was common practice for an artisan to build two houses with a mutual wall. He would live in one and rent the other.

5 613-626 Sharp Street are new buildings described as infill development. Their purpose is to provide new housing in consistent character and scale with 'he old.

6 715 Sharp Street is now the Church of the Lord Jesus Christ and is used by one of the Reformed Groups. It was built in 1889 by the Methodists.

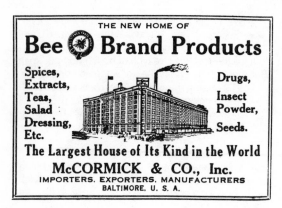
► In the 1820s the African Colonization Society was formed with plans to return free blacks in Maryland to establish a new colony in Liberia, Africa. While the colony was formed the overall plan failed. A lawyer named Daniel Raymond had joined Tyson in the leadership role and he said at this time: "The African Race is effectively planted in this country and will remain here until the last day....They are here and have as much right here as the whites."[3]

The Sharp Street United Methodist Church was formed in this neighborhood by and for blacks in early 1800. The Church has moved to 1206 Etting Street.

► In 1865, at the end of the Civil War, the Baltimore Association for the Moral and Educational Development of the Colored People was formed. They founded seven schools. The City Council contributed $10,000. The State Legislature and the Council of Christian churches refused to become involved. Rabbi Szold made a donation "mindful of the captivity of our people in Egypt." Black citizens and Quakers gave $5,000, Friends in England sent £750.[4]

► Street names have never been changed. Lee Street was named for "Lighthorse Harry" the father of Robert E. Lee. His actual name was Richard Henry Lee and he served as a General in the American Revolution. Isaac Barre was an early colonialist. Hanover honors the Hanovarian line of King George III.

7 The large building on the west side of Sharp Street is The Federal Reserve Bank.

Current residents in the area are praising the "Federal Reserve" for protecting them from the threat of intrusion by some vague, but scene-destructive building such as a high rise hotel. And they are most grateful for the tasteful and colorful landscaping.

The building was completed in 1981. When the foundations were dug the "other side" of Sharp Street was exposed. Basements of early houses and many relics of everyday life were scattered throughout the rubble. More than 3,000 artifacts were identified and catalogued. They are now on display in the lobby of the bank. It's an interesting testimony to the lifestyle of the first Baltimoreans. You are invited to browse. The bank is open Monday-Friday, 9 am - 4 pm.

Hopkins/Chesney Archives

A public health student making a home visit.

▶ Mrs. Taylor will sell her house for $200,000 cash and "no questions asked." But she really does not want to sell. "How long does money last anyway?" She came to Baltimore from North Carolina with her husband in 1946. They rented this property and then bought it in the "nineteens and fifties."
Mrs. Taylor says she used to carry fresh vegetables but she's "a little on the lazy side now" so she carries "quick snacks of ice cream, sodas and all kinds of potato chips."

T. Chandlee

Geneva Taylor, 811 Sharp Street.

▶ The Otterbein reflects the wishes of today's wealthy buyer. The houses are an investment — not a store place for family histories as our mother's house was. And there are no large back yards because people today don't want to be bothered with caring for them.

▶ Inside, the houses are quite modern. Many have double height living rooms, skylights, large elaborate kitchens, bathrooms with sunken Jacuzzi bathtubs, marble, mirrors, multi-shower heads for massage, and master bedrooms with a fireplace.

8 811 Sharp Street is ½ a block off the route of the tour. It is the store and home of Geneva Taylor and her family. It's the only place in Baltimore, that I know, where you can still buy Tootsie Rolls and bubble gum for a penny. Hot balls are up to 2¢ here, and Sugar Daddys cost a nickel. Mrs. Taylor is a "hold out" from the Otterbein expansion. Have a snowball or a Coke and talk with her.

9 Let's return to the church and walk down Hughes Street to the green space. Turn left. These small parks were a part of the original home-steading plan. Trees and grass were planted by the city and their maintenance is still the responsi-bility of the city. Flower beds are the work of individual residents.

We'll cross Hill Street and continue on the green. Note the church on your right. It is now attractive condominiums.

10 York Alley is a typical small cobblestone area where those who worked for people in the larger houses once lived.

11 We emerge beside 123 Lee Street. This was once St. Joseph's Roman Catholic Church. (1915-1973) which was torn down during the home-steading. Today there are three individual "fill-in" houses. On your right, at 118 Lee Street, is the house where the priests for the church once lived.

12 We'll turn left. 125 Lee Street is where the nuns lived. 137 W. Lee Street was built in 1805 by Benjamin Berry, a captain in Washington's artillery, and later a brickmaker. He, together with his brother, John, were members of the first City Council.

13 Let's cross and walk east down Lee Street. Not much research has been done on the original owners of these houses. 132 W. Lee Street is the house made from the Tepper Hotel.

124 W. Lee Street is thought to be the oldest house in the area. It was built in 1792 by Matthew Paulson, a ship's captain.

► *The new homesteaders were yuppies, single or married, and older couples whose children had left home. It was a worthy investment. The housing sells currently for $150,000-$400,000.*

► *Otterbein is gradually losing the young couples with children because they want to live near schools.*

► *Property for sale signs seem to stay in place longer than other neighborhoods. Maybe that's because there is a resistance to lowering the price.*

T. Chandlee

Recent Otterbein homesteading.

14 We'll turn left at Hanover Street. Before doing so, glance at the park on the south side of the street. It is an attractive one, perfect for babies and nannies. The wheel was once used as a street car turn-around to go back when it had reached the end of the line.

The west side of Hanover Street is the eastern border of the homestead area. The condos on the east side of the street are called "wraparounds" because they adjoin the rehab section.

15 Turn left onto Welcome Alley and stroll west-ward. The feeling of the entire Otterbein section seems to be one of an established well-heeled community. The quiet belies its closeness to the business section of Baltimore City.

16 We'll turn right at Sharp Street and return to Barre where we began. If you have time wander down Barre Street. It contains some very nice houses.

1. Old Otterbein Rectory
2. Old Otterbein Church
3. Moses Sheppard House
4. 206 W. Pratt cast-iron front
5. Bromo Seltzer Building
6. Sigmund Sonneborn & Company
7. Isaac Hamburg Company
8. A.S. Abell Building
9. Original Eutaw Savings Bank
10. Second Eutaw Savings Bank
11. Old European Delicatessen
12. Lexington Market
13. General Dispensary Building
14. Old Westminster Church/Burial Grounds
15. Pascault Row
16. Pine Street Police Station

A. Community block grant housing
B. H.L. Mencken's Birthplace
C. Poe House
17. Old St. Paul's Cemetery
18. Davidge Hall
19. Babe Ruth House
20. Camden Station

▶ The early flavor of this area vanished long ago, but the names of the streets remain as testimony to the past. Conway was a Marylander who opposed the Stamp Act, passed by the British Parliament in 1765. Horatio Sharpe was a respected Proprietary Governor of Maryland from 1753-1759.

▶ When the rectory first opened it was used as a house for widowed women because Bishop Otterbein was still alive and he preferred to remain in a small cottage in front of the church yard where he had always lived. Otterbein was a religious zealot who came from Prussia to the New World in 1752. He was greatly attracted by the teachings of Bishop Francis Asbury so he came to Baltimore and established the German Reformed Church on this spot in 1774. The philosophy of the Reformed Church contained strong Methodist learnings. By 1968 all the ideological differences had become reconciled and Old Otterbein Church was joined with the United Methodist.

R. Pryzbylowski

Bells from Bremen in Old Otterbein Church.

▶ There was a major influx of German immigrants into the Port of Baltimore during the late seventeenth and early eighteenth centuries because Baltimore ships were going into German ports with wheat and tobacco. In the belfry of Old Otterbein Church are bells which were brought from Bremen to Baltimore in 1789. When a ship full of new German citizens landed at the dock, which was then at the foot of Conway Street, the bells would be rung to summon everyone to welcome them.

This walk begins on Conway Street just west of the Sheraton Inner Harbor Hotel. On your right is the rectory for the old Otterbein United Methodist Church.

1 The rectory was built in 1811 and is the oldest orginal parsonage in use by any United Methodist Church in the United States. The grass, flowers and trees which surround the rectory and the church are planted and pruned by the Guilford Garden Club. The Club considers this to be one of its most cherished responsibilities.

T. Chandlee

Tracery pattern in the windows of the Old Otterbein Church.

2 Old Otterbein Church was built in 1785 at a cost of $5,000. It is the oldest church building in Baltimore City. The builder was a local carpenter named Jacob Small. See the lovely windows. The decorative openwork is known as tracery and represents an architectural style used in Europe by the early Germans. The use of plain glass in lieu of stained is indicative of German frugality.

The tower was added in 1789, paid for by monies raised from a lottery. Small was criticized for its squat Teutonic appearance. He is said to have snorted at his critics stating,

"When you see the bill you will find the steeple high enough,"

The small brick building in the northern portion of the courtyard was built in 1872 to be a parish hall and Sunday School.

The church is open every Sunday at 12 noon for tourists. It is open on Saturdays from 10 am to 4 pm April-October. Phone 685-4703 for more details.

▶ *The purpose of our tour is to call attention to the historical aspects of the city. So we'll not take time to explore the new.*

T. Chandlee

Iron front put on buildings in 1888.

▶ *In 1851 the use of cast iron was introduced into architectural design and construction. It was the beginning of modern day structural steel architecture. The concept of metal as an important component of a building was alien and unacceptable to many Victorian conservatives. For years its use was treated with contempt by those known as classicists . . .*

▶ *In 1865 this area was the cultural center of the German Community. The Concordia Opera House was here and Dickens came from London to read from his works.*
   Gradually it changed to become the center for manufacturing (primarily clothing) in Baltimore.

As you leave Old Otterbein Church on your right is the Baltimore Convention Center completed in 1979. On your left is Festival Hall completed in 1986.

3 We'll turn west onto Pratt Street. Look at the building on the corner of Pratt and Liberty Streets. Notice the boxy proportions, the gable roof, the dormer windows, and the Flemish bond brickwork. These are all distinctive elements of the Federal style town house. This house was built in 1796. In 1826 it became the home of Moses Sheppard, a merchant, a Quaker, and a man so interested in the problems of the mentally ill that he willed $157,000 for the building of a private hospital near Towson, Maryland to treat and cure such patients.

From 1857-1920 the property was rented to Jacob and Abraham Speer as a cobbler's shop. Then it housed the Katzenstein Family and their art business until 1987.

4 206 W. Pratt Street is an interesting building with an iron front and cast iron hoods above the upper floor windows. Such fronting was the grand-father of prefabricated housing. Its use was decorative as well as economical and it became "the rage" during the latter part of the nineteenth century. Iron fronts were made in Baltimore by the Bartlett-Hayward Company, which for a period of time, was the largest producer of architectural ironwork in the nation. There are few examples of this cast-iron elegance left in the city. This particular front was put on this building in 1888 when three town houses were made into a warehouse. P. J. Crickett's Restaurant began here in 1980.

Let's turn right onto Eutaw Street and proceed northward. It's obvious that the original grandeur of this section has been lost, but a few buildings remain which reflect the past and they are what we shall see.

▶ *Isaac Emerson was a druggest who came to Baltimore from North Carolina. The formula for Bromo Seltzer was one he developed while experimenting with drugs which would help his first wife's migraine headaches. Mt. Bromo is a volcano in Java. Emerson took the name, patented his formula and made a fortune. When his first wife divorced him, he immediately married a woman with Vanderbilt connections and moved into a model dairy farm in the elite social world of the Green Spring Valley.*

The Bromo Seltzer Tower with the original rotating bottle on top.

5 21 S. Eutaw Street is called the Bromo Seltzer Tower by old-time Baltimoreans. It was built in 1911 by "Captain" Isaac Emerson to contain the offices of his drug company. The tower is an exact copy of the Palazzo Vecchio in Florence, Italy. When it was completed it was the tallest and most ostentatious building in Baltimore. The clock is supposed to be the largest four-dial gravity clock in the world. Bromo Seltzer lost its lure, even for hang-overs, and in 1968 the building was given to the city to be the home of the Mayor's Advisory Committee on Art and Culture. The large firehouse you see on Baltimore Street replaced a portion of the administration offices.

6 10-14 S. Eutaw Street built in 1850 was the clothing firm of Sigmund Sonneborn & Company. It was the largest clothing firm in Baltimore, the best organized and paid the best salaries.

The firm's specialties were police uniforms and sleepwear for the general public.

7 18-20 S. Eutaw was the second factory for the Isaac Hamburger Company, the city's oldest retail clothing firm. The company was organized in 1850 and we will see its current store when we walk on Charles Street.

8 The southeast corner of Baltimore and Eutaw Street is the A. S. Abell Building, a wonderful Victorian warehouse, designed by George A. Fredrick in 1878. It was the first large loft to be built specifically to accommodate clothing. Note the use of bluestone, white marble, and terra cotta.[1] A. S. Abell was the owner of the Baltimore Sun and a man with a taste for flair.

▶ The Baltimore City Fire Department was not organized until 1858. Before this date fires were fought by two groups: men paid by insurance companies and/or volunteer fire companies. Neither were reliable. Insurance companies like the Equitable Society, provided both insurance for the house and the men to extinguish the fire. Each company had its own "mark" which was placed on the outside wall of an insuree's house. This "mark" was an iron plaque containing the insurance company's symbol, such as the two golden hands of the Equitable Society. With the insurance company's mark in place, should a fire occur one knew which company was responsible for squelching the flames. Not that it did much good. When an alarm was sounded, hired firefighters from **ALL** the insurance companies responded. But only the men who saw **THEIR** company's mark on the house attacked the fire. All the other firefighters either watched the house burn down or razzed men from the rival company who tried to save it.

In time, four volunteer companies were formed in Baltimore City. These men were paid for the fires they fought, but they were much more interested in fighting among themselves. Frequently fires were started in order to have a race to the scene and battle among the men.

During the 1700's the best way to gain revenge against an enemy was to burn his house down. Legally this was acceptable — even praiseworthy, in spite of the danger to adjoining properties.

Baltimore Equitable Society

FOR INSURING HOUSES AND FURNITURE FROM LOSS OR DAMAGE BY FIRE.

S. E. Cor. Eutaw and Fayette Sts.

Incorporated 1794.

WILTON SNOWDEN, Treasurer.

HARRY E. RAWLINGS, Secretary.

9 21 N. Eutaw Street built in 1857, is the Eutaw Savings Bank. The Baltimore Equitable Society moved into the building in 1889. Not much has changed. Step inside and see bank tellers still working behind iron mesh above an old bank counter. There is an interesting collection of old fire fighting equipment in the second floor museum and some rare fire marks line the walls of the treasurer's office.[2] The Equitable's mark contains two golden hands in a clasp over the date 1794.

Open Monday-Friday 9 am-3 pm.

MD Historical Society

The Baltimore Equitable Society in 1900.

10 Directly across Eutaw Street is the second Eutaw Savings Bank built in 1887.

11 117 N. Eutaw Street is the Old European Delicatessen, Inc. owned by a German family named Nemela. They make their own hot dogs, sausage, and a variety of meat loafs. Their food is "old world" and we recommend stopping in.

▶ *In 1780 the ground where the market stands today was the outskirts of Baltimore Town. It was a steep grassy hill where gypsies camped and innocent children and slaves were raped. It was part of the estate of John Eager Howard who sold it to the Town in order to put a stop to the promiscuous activities. The Howard family still collects ground rent. The market was formed to be an outlet for the flour and grain which was brought to Baltimore by German farmers from Western Maryland. Soon other farmers were polishing apples, scrubbing carrots, and washing spinach in order to attract customers. As Baltimore grew so did the market. There was an air of intimacy and personal interest between vendor and customer. They were on a first name basis. Special items were saved for special people. Butchers trimmed meat and cut roasts and steaks to order. Poultry men cut the head off a hen and tied the feet together so the bird could hang on the side of a basket. And fishermen brought their catch from the Chesapeake Bay. As late as 1949 the market was a series of wooden sheds without refrigeration or screens for insect control. On March 25, 1949 it burned away, much to the relief of the Health Department.*

12 Across Eutaw Street is the new entrance to the old Lexington Market. Touted locally as the most famous market in the world, it was 200 years old in 1982. Let's wander through it. Many of the meat and poultry stalls are operated by descendants of the original families. Most of the vegetable vendors were once Italian. Today they are Korean. Faidley's Seafood is an old family business. Like raw oysters? Stop and have some, fresh from the Chesapeake Bay.

LOMBARD STREET.

S.E. COR.

N.

OUR BLOCK.

THE

W. B.C.BIBB E.

STOVE COMPANY.

BALTIMORE, MD.

RANGES, FURNACES, STOVES, FIRE PLACE HEATERS.

S

LIGHT STREET.

ELLICOTT STREET.

BALDERSTON STREET.

13 We'll leave the market at the Paca Street exit and walk south to Fayette Street. The square building on the northwest corner was built in 1911 to be the Baltimore General Dispensary and was in use as such until 1977. It was the model for the era. Clinical areas on the first floor were divided into two sections: one for white patients and one for black patients. The treatment rooms on the second floor were small and curtained which provided a privacy for the medical examination of charity patients that had never existed before.

The Baltimore General Dispensary Foundation was formed in 1801 and was located at 127 E. Baltimore Street. Money for its support came from State lotteries and from fines imposed by the Sheriff's office on persons keeping houses of ill fame. Baltimore's most prominent doctors gave their time free of charge.

▶ Westminster Presbyterian Church was built forty-five years (1851-52) after the cemetery so the rear end is raised and you can enter into what is known as the catacombs. This is currently a popular place to visit on Halloween night. Several of the vaults have burst open and you see the bones of early Baltimoreans.

Pratt Library

Westminster Church, the burial ground for Edgar Allan Poe, 15 generals and 200 officers of the American Revolution.

▶ It's a gloomy cemetery with family vaults that look more like ovens than peaceful resting places, but thats the way they did things in those days. The intention was to mourn the brevity of life and to celebrate the eternity of the spirit.

▶ The medical school of the University of Maryland was a threat to "eternal rest." In 1815, it was illegal for the city to supply cadavers from its morgue for teaching purposes so medical students were on the lookout for funeral processions. They would rent a horse and buggy, would enter the cemetery after dark, take the corpse from the grave, prop it between them — like a drunken comrade — and would be off to the anatomy lab at Davidge Hall.

▶ After World War II, the church lost its congregation to the suburbs. In the late 1970's the Westminster Preservation Trust was formed. Tours arranged by calling 328-7228. Admission fee.

14 Let's walk west one block on Fayette Street to the Westminster Church located on the southeast corner at Greene Street. This is sometimes referred to as the most historic 3/4 acre in America because 15 generals and over 200 officers and enlisted men from the American Revolution and the War of 1812 are buried here. So is Edgar Allan Poe. Poe's family lot is behind the church, up on a small knoll, but note the monument on your right as you enter the cemetery yard. Twenty-six years after Poe's death in 1849 the city moved his body and placed it in this monument together with that of his young wife Virginia and his stepmother, Mrs. Clemm. There are often floral wreaths and flowers here from foreign and local admirers. Nickels and dimes are tossed around the base as gestures of good luck. This is the epitome of irony. Poe's fame and his luck when he was alive were zilch.

T. Chandlee

Poe's grave in the Westminster Cemetery.

The burial yard belonged to the First Presbyterian Church. The iron carriage entrance which faces onto Greene Street and five of the largest and oldest burial vaults were the work of Maximilian Godefroy. In the Federal Gazette, September 15, 1815, Godefroy invited prospective clients to see his work, which included these vaults: the mausoleum for John O'Donnell, a pyramid for James Calhoun (the first mayor of Baltimore) and James Buchanan, a pseudo temple for Robert and William Smith, and a vault on a plot owned by Cumberland Dugan.[3]

Many of the tombs have vents in them. The purpose was to provide a means for communication in case someone should be buried alive — by mistake, or course.

▶ William Patterson was a 14-year-old Irish orphan who landed in Philadelphia in 1766. By 1778 when he came to make a home in Baltimore, he had such a fortune from real estate and shipping that he was described as the second richest man in Maryland (the first was Charles Carroll of Carrollton.)[5] His daughter, Betsy, was born in 1785. On Christmas Eve, 1803, Betsy was married to Jerome Bonaparte, the brother of Napoleon. She was quite a beauty, but Napoleon was not pleased with the match. Neither was Mr. Patterson. He sent Betsy to the Springs to cool her passion, but she returned saying that she would rather be married to Jerome Bonaparte for one hour than be the wife of another man for an eternity.

A witness at the wedding wrote:

> All the clothes she wore might be put into my pocket. Her dress was muslin richly em-broidered, but of extremely fine texture. Beneath her dress she wore but a single garment.[4]

In 1804 Napoleon was made Emperor of France and ordered his brother to return "without your little girl." Betsy went anyway, she was denied admittance into France, so she went on to England where she gave birth to a son, Jerome Napoleon Bonaparte. Napoleon had had the marriage annulled and she never saw her lover again. Her friend, Henrietta Pascault, married a member of Jerome's retinue and lived happily in France, the daughter-in-law of a wealthy French banker.[5]

Pratt Library

The 600 block of W. Lexington Street, Pascault Row.

15 Now we'll walk one block north on Greene Street to Lexington. On your left at the end of the 600 block of Lexington Street is Pascault Row. This is an especially fine row of eight town houses which were designed in 1802 for a Baltimore merchant named Louis Pascault. The houses represent Federal architecture at its dignified best.

Pascault was also the father of two of Baltimore's most popular belles. It was at a dinner party given by Mr. Pascault for his daughter, Henrietta, that Betsy Patterson was introduced to Jerome Bonaparte.

The University of Maryland now owns these houses and they have been renovated for student housing.

Pratt Library

Lexington Market in 1926.

16 Glance to the west and see the unique, isolated building a block ahead on the left. This is the old Pine Street Police Station, built in 1871. It's a superb example of high Victorian Gothic design. It was saved from demolition in 1980 by the Commission for Historical and Architectural Preservation and is an historic landmark.[6] In 1983 it was traded by the city to the University of Maryland in return for the Mencken House.

The walk from here to the Poe House is not a good one at the present time because of the shifting neighborhood. So we recommend that walkers proceed south to Redwood Street. If you are in a car or wish to know about this specific section of Baltimore please refer to the opposite page.

Pratt Library

Portrait of Edgar Allan Poe by Thomas C. Corner.

▶ *Edgar Allan Poe is one of the major figures in the history of American literature, but it was the French poet Baudelaire who recognized his genius and announced it to the overseas world years before many people in the United States knew who he was. This is an example of the way things were with Poe. His life was a series of traumatic events. He flunked out of the University of Virginia, his stepfather disowned him, his wife died of tuberculosis three years after they were married. His agent did nothing to publicize his works in America and he pocketed for himself the few royalties which did trickle in. Poe lived the majority of his life in Richmond, Virginia and in New York City. His health was never good. In September, 1849, he was found wandering delerious in downtown Baltimore. He died four days after he was admitted to what is now Church Hospital.*

Head west on Lexington Street to Amity.

A In the late 1970's Baltimore City designated a parcel of monies known as Community Block Grant Funds to several private agencies. The hope was that this type of public partnership would provide a stimulus for further revitalization of declining neighborhoods and would serve as an example to other impoverished areas. The program had one essential requirement: the reconstructed dwellings were to be sold or rented only by low to moderate income persons who were capable of assuming responsibility for the maintenance of their property. Residents were to serve on the board of the developing agency and assist in developing guidelines for the supervision and enforcement of maintenance criteria.

The end result was that the original character of the area remained unchanged.

B The 800 block of Lexington Street illustrates the full three story brick house which local builders began to construct about 1850. Henry Mencken was born in 1880 at 813 Lexington Street.

This entire area is associated with the growth and development of the railroad.

Turning the corner onto Amity Street we see the style of row house which was built in the 1830's and 1840's They provided a practical living area for blue collar people with large families plus a boarder or two.

C At the end of this block, on the left, is the small house where Edgar Allan Poe lived with his aunt Mary Clemm and her daughter, Virginia, from 1830 to 1833. He subsequently married Virginia when she was just fourteen years old. Note the little garden in the rear which is maintained by the Ednor Gardens Garden Club. The house is not open on a regular basis. Call 396-7932 for information. Admission is free.

Pratt Library

The Poe house on Amity Street.

▶ *In 1812 the teaching of medicine as a profession was not yet recognized as an essential process. It was against the law to dissect bodies, yet every student had to know the human anatomy and its organic functioning by heart. Because of the proximity of Westminster Cemetery, Frank, the janitor for Davidge Hall soon became known as Frank, the body snatcher. Cadavers became so plentiful that one instructor shipped three to a colleague in Maine. They were stored in barrels full of whiskey to preserve them. Frank was in charge of this procedure and he made a little money on the side by selling shots of whiskey to students who sipped it on the way up steps which led to the laboratories.*

▶ *Ultimately, the public benefited. The University of Maryland was the first medical school in the country to make anatomical dissection compulsory, the first to use biopsy and the microscope to diagnose malignancy, and the first to include the study and practice of gross and microscopic pathology.*

17 Mid-block on Redwood Street is an early cemetery for Old St. Paul Protestant Episcopal Church. It was actually the third cemetery for this Church but it contains graves of parish members who died in the seventeenth century because their remains were transferred here when earlier burial grounds became inadequate.

At the time when this land was purchased, in 1800, the area was still countryside. It became the most fashionable address for burial in Baltimore. John Eager Howard is here, Samuel Chase, a signer of the Declaration of Independence, Thorowgood Smith, second mayor of Baltimore and many who were prominent enough to have their names used for the streets of Baltimore.

Open on Saturday. For information phone: 685-3404.

Now we'll skirt the cemetery and walk down Lombard Street to Greene.

18 On the northeast corner of Greene Street at Pratt is Davidge Hall. This is the oldest medical school building in use for that purpose in the United States. It was designed in 1812 by Robert Cary Long, a carpenter who became an architect. With a minimum of formal training, Long completed this building and topped it with a dome which spans 60 feet. His model was the Philadelphia medical school building designed by Benjamin Latrobe the distinguished architect of the time. Latrobe's dome had a span of only 30 feet. Long also managed to place one round lecture room on top of another without allowing the support system to be visible and thus distracting. The man was a genius and we'll see more of his work later in downtown Baltimore.

The University of Maryland was the fifth medical school to be organized in the United States. The hall was named for John Beale Davidge, the first dean. Prior to its opening classes were held in professors' homes.

The building has just been restored. Tours including its medical museum may be arranged by calling: 328-6975.

▶ *It is fortunate that baseball was a popular sport among the brothers who staffed St. Mary's Training School. They discovered and nourished the great talent of George Herman Ruth. When he was barely eighteen, Ruth left the School to go with the Orioles to their Florida training camp. He was so unworldly and naive that he was dubbed "Babe-in-the-woods" by his teammates. He was seeing many things for the first time: elevators, head waiters, burlesque shows. His exuberance was uncontrollable. The nickname "Babe" stuck with him throughout his career. He was an enthusiastic and supportive team member who spent a great deal of time with children, especially those he felt that he could help. He did marry, but he was famous for his love of women, a good party and abundant food and drink.*

Babe Ruth Museum

Babe Ruth.

19 Let's go west on Pratt Street for a block and turn left onto Emory Street. This seems to be the best time to visit the Babe Ruth House.

216 Emory Street is where Babe Ruth was born, the son of German immigrants. Legend says he was an orphan, but this is not true. He was a bad kid and he was placed in St. Mary's Training School because he needed the disciplinary program offered there.

The house is furnished in the style of the late 1800's. The Ruths were poor so it's doubtful that they could have afforded such a fancy parlor. But there's some wonderful memorabilia from the Babe's baseball years. His New York Yankee uniform and the furniture from his New York apartment are there. Also, a museum for the Baltimore Oriole Baseball Club. The house is open daily from 10am-4pm. Phone 727-1539. Admission fee.

▶ Trains to and from the north ended at the President Street Station which is three blocks west of here. Cars were pulled by horses along Pratt Street to solidify the connection and enable passengers to continue on their way. But this break was a serious problem at the time of the Civil War. In February, 1861 Abraham Lincoln came through here one night before he was expected and "sneaked" via a private carriage from President Street to Camden on his way to Washington to be inaugurated President of the United States. In April, 1861 Southern sympathizers attacked the 6th Massachusetts Infantry as it made the transfer between stations and caused the first bloodshed in the Civil War. Lincoln came again, on his way to Gettysburg to give his famous speech, and he came once more, in 1865, in a coffin. His body lay in state in Baltimore for three hours before going on to Illinois to be buried.

Ironically, the body of John Wilkes Booth, the assassin of Lincoln, was also brought to the station in 1869. His family owned a plot in Greenmount Cemetery and the body of John Wilkes Booth was buried there in an unmarked grave.

Pratt Library

20 We'll walk down Emory Street, turn left at Portland and cross Greene Street to Camden Street. The red brick building on your right is the Camden Station, built in 1857 for the Baltimore and Ohio Railroad. It was designed to be a showcase, comparable to King's Cross and Paddington Stations in London. Originally there were towers atop each end, and in the center, but they were found to be structurally unsound and were removed a few years after the station was completed. When it opened, Camden was the northernmost station of the B&O. All of the company's general offices were housed here. So were runaway slaves. It was a major link in the Underground Railroad. We don't know if it was intentional, but there are a series of catacombs beneath the station and a tunnel which is rumored to go all the way south to Fort McHenry. Harriet Tubman, the leader of the underground railroad hid her parents here in 1857, until she could find a way to get them into Canada.

In 1912, the National Democratic Convention was held in Baltimore. The Railroad Company spent $1,000,000 making improvements to the station so that William Jennings Bryan and Woodrow Wilson could arrive in the style appropriate to their ambitions.

Across from the Camden Station is Old Otterbein Church, the place where you began and now will end this tour.

Camden Station around 1912.

NOTES Southwest Baltimore

LEXINGTON ST.

CAREY ST.

C

A

B

FAYETTE ST.

CALHOUN ST.

STRICKER ST.

GILMORE ST.

5

8

HOLLINS ST.

4

6

LOMBARD ST

7

LEMMON ST.

CAREY ST.

A

WASHINGTON BLVD.

184

1. *B&O Roundhouse Museum*
2. *Houses with formstone fronts*
A. *Church of St. Peter the Apostle*
B. *Rectory*
C. *Convent*
D. *Lithuanian Hall*
3. *Hollins Market*
4. *Enoch Pratt Library, Branch 2*
5. *H.L. Mencken House*
6. *Union Square*

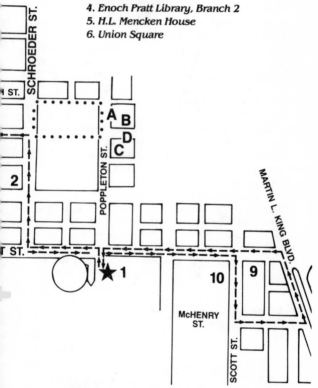

7. *Lemmon Street*
8. *Carey Street*
9. *Barre Circle*
10. *Bartlett-Hayward Company*
A. *Waverly Terrace*
B. *Canby Row*
C. *St. Luke's Episcopal Church*
A. *Mount Clare Mansion and Carroll Park*

IMPACT OF THE RAILROAD

*W*e need to stop here for a minute in order to consider the impact of the Baltimore and Ohio Railroad on Baltimore City.

One of the major worries of a city which is a port is **HOW** to get the product to and from the water. In the 1800s overland travel was by horse and wagon. This was so incredibly slow that methods for developing inland waterways began to be studied.[1]

By 1820 Philadelphia and Baltimore were working together with plans to develop the Susquehanna and Potomac River routes. A local architect named Robert Mills (who had planned the Washington Monument) designed an elaborate plan for a series of canals via waterways throughout the state which would bring trade from both of these rivers into Baltimore. Said Mills:

"Baltimore is destined to become the emporium of the eastern section of the Union — provided proper exertions are made to secure the advantages offered …Shall we remain passive spectators?…Shall our energies sleep?"[2]

The cost of his plan was estimated to be $2,000,000. True to form, Baltimoreans panicked and the state appointed two commissions: one to study access to the Potomac, the other to study access to the Susquehanna. In 1823 a commission report recommended a plan for a canal which would involve a system of locks, but which would eventually provide for

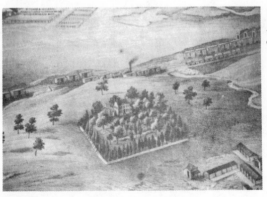

Sache map

James McCubbin Carroll leased Mount Clare property as right-of-way to the railroad.

IMPACT OF THE RAILROAD

an entryway from the Potomac River into Baltimore. This plan would cost $1,000,000.

Again there was panic and this time the city appointed a committee with specific instructions to "find a cheaper way."[3]

Meanwhile, Philadelphia and the State of Pennsylvania began an extensive system of state waterworks most of which would benefit only themselves.

Baltimore splurged and spent $50,000 to improve navigation in the Susquehanna. The Maryland legislature approved a proposal to build the Chesapeake and Potomac Canal, but it did not include a feasible connection from the canal to Baltimore.

In 1825 the Erie Canal was finished in northern New York State so trade from Canada and the northwest, which had previously gone south via the Mississippi, was diverted into New York City thereby pushing the operations of that port far ahead of Philadelphia and Baltimore.

By 1827 Baltimore was still financially inhibited and very close to financial embarrassment.

Then a man named Evan Thomas returned from England where he had seen a mining railroad. This was described as an engine driven by steam which pulled cars on a perfectly straight track from one place to another. His brother, Philip Thomas was a banker and had some influence with the little group of financiers who would come up with the money if they considered it to their advantage to do so. The group included Alexander Brown, William Patterson, Robert Oliver and Charles Carroll of Carrollton.

The Thomas brothers were able to sell them on the idea of building a railroad. Philip Thomas was chosen to be the first president. A charter was drawn up and accepted by the Maryland legislature on February 27, 1827.

"The railroad will be the very thing to redeem Baltimoreans from their embarrassments, and restore them to their original rights and inheritance.

"...Baltimore will yet become the first city in the nation." So spoke John H.B. Latrobe.[4]

Army engineers were hired to dig the beds for the tracks. There were two goals: the Ohio River in the west, the Susquehanna River in the north

They *had* to use Pratt Street so that freight cars could reach the harbor, but the people of Baltimore were adamant against the use of steam engines on their busiest street. They were so opposed that they sent a statement to the United States Congress which said:

> Every water pump, hydrant, lamp post, awning post, tree, and feeding trough on the street would have to be removed. The horses would be scared, mothers would be unable to allow children to cross the street to go to school and no lady would be able to shop.[5]

Knowledge relating to the use of steam was limited. It was expected that horses would have to be used in the countryside to ease engines around curves or up hills.

As a result a law was written which stated that only horses could pull railroad cars between the Camden Station and the one on President Street and to the loading docks. The law remained in effect for years after the use of steam was an accepted fact.

On August 28, 1830 Peter Cooper took his engine, named the Tom Thumb, on its successful run between Baltimore and Ellicott City and railroad history began in fact. Cooper proved three things:

1. A steam engine could pull a car uphill.
2. A steam engine could pull a car around curves.
3. A steam engine could pull many times its own weight.

A man named Ross Winans came to Baltimore from New Jersey to sell some horses to the railroad. He became so intrigued with what he saw that he stayed and made such innovative contributions to the development of steam locomotives and coaches that

IMPACT OF THE RAILROAD

he was invited to Russia by the Czar to design a railroad which would run from Moscow to St. Petersburg.

On it went. The railroad became an answer not only to Baltimore's problem of inadequate transportation from port to market, but also to that of the nation. For a while the economy of the city swelled with new jobs.

Then the city lost the railroad. In February, 1896, only sixty-nine years after the charter had been accepted by the Maryland legislature, the Baltimore and Ohio went into the hands of New York receivers. It was bankrupt and even though there was a quick rebound of capital value, Baltimore had lost control of it. The new owners were a Chicago group named Armour.[6]

The reasons for the loss again reflect the city's insular character.

B&O Archives

Railroad yards and roundhouse.

▶ *The inner core of the industry here collapsed soon after the initial impetus. When Winans left, his prolific shops were closed and his employees were put out of work. Philadelphia quickly began to breed engine manufacturers. The State of Pennsylvania built track and there was little or no exchange of goods and services between Baltimore railroad shops and those in Philadelphia.*

Local investors supported the iron and coal industries in Cumberland as opposed to local firms.

▶ *Baltimore capitalists were, as usual, ultraconservative. Money was recycled only in a small circle which did not allow for expansion into outside markets.*

▶ *The land west of the Mississippi was just beginning to be settled so commercial markets were still limited to the eastern seaboard and the south.*

▶ *This portion of southwest Baltimore developed with the railroad. In 1830 there was an influx of Irish into the port of Baltimore, and more Germans. These people dug the railroad beds, laid the track, repaired it, loaded freight, acted as conductors, porters, fireman, engineers and ticket agents.*

At their peak, the B&O shops employed 1,000, Bartlett Hayward 350, and other locomotive works and foundries 100-150.[7]

1 Now we'll begin this tour at the B&O Roundhouse on Pratt Street at Poppleton. The Roundhouse was built in 1883 to be an industrial building in
which passenger cars could be built and repaired. It
was known as a car shop. The shape was considered
practical, allowing for a turntable in the center and
optimal space for parking and storing of cars around
the sides. Notice that the sign over the entrance says
Mount Clare Station. This building is an exact repro-
duction of the first railroad station ever built in America
and thought to be the first in the world. It is located on
the same spot as the first.

   The museum opened in July, 1953. It contains the
most comprehensive collection of historic locomotives
and railroad memorabilia in America.

   It is open Wednesday-Sunday from 10 am-4 pm.
Admission fee.

Mount Clare Station in 1830.

2 We'll walk north on Schroeder Street to Hollins
and turn left. You may wonder about the artificial
rock fronts, you see on some of the houses you are
passing. It is called formstone and is considered a
sacrilege by preservationists because it covers the
original brick, but actually the bricks used by blue-
collar workers to build their homes were porous. The
formstone is a weatherizer. It came into vogue after
World War II and was expensive to apply. Only the
more prosperous could afford it, hence it lent an aura
of prestige to the home it protected.

▶ *The church was built in order to provide service to the large group of Irish railroad workers who had moved into this area. It is constructed on a bed of granite from Ellicott City quarries brought to Baltimore by the new railroad.*

For many years the church conducted the second largest Catholic school in Baltimore.

In 1968, the church's beautiful frescos and side altars were destroyed by the Vatican II reactionaries. A free standing altar was installed.

▶*Note the Greek Temple design. By 1842, the mania for Ancient Greek architecture had reached its peak in Europe and in America. No valid architect would consider any other form.*

▶ *The Lithuanians came to Baltimore in 1902-1905 and again in 1945, after World War II when Russia absorbed their country.*

Most of them were tailors by trade and went to work in the garment district. They work hard to keep their wonderful culture and its characteristics alive. There are national folk dance groups which practice weekly in the Hall. Crafts are on display and may be purchased.

Little Lithuanian DETOUR

A Walk east on Hollins to Poppleton Street to the Church of St. Peter the Apostle, designed by Robert Cary Long, Jr. in 1842. It contains some nice Bavarian stained glass windows and a 90 year-old organ built by the Baltimore organ maker Henry Nieman. It is the largest of its kind still in use. Stop by the rectory or phone 685-5044 to gain admittance to the church.

B 848 Hollins Street is the rectory — also designed by Long in 1849. At the time it was considered the last word in modern architecture.

C 13 S. Poppleton is the convent staffed by the first foundation of the Sisters of Mercy. They still provide preschool classes for the community.

D 851 Hollins Street is Lithuanian Hall which has been in existence for 61 years. It is a cultural center with a charming museum where wood carvings, decorated eggs, and exquisite Christmas tree ornaments made from straw are on display. Dinner is served once a week on Friday evenings and you may go if you make a reservation in advance. Call 685-5787. And try their national drink. It's a potent liqueur made from honey and named Viryta.

▶ The market and the church served as the centers for social activities in every neighborhood in Baltimore. The aura of the Hollins Market in its heyday was quite earthy. The vendors were flirtatious and bold in their attempts to attract customers. There were additional stalls on the street and a wonderful sense of "old worldliness" with flowers displayed everywhere.

▶ This was such an intensely German area that for years the German language was taught and spoken in the local schools. English was studied as a secondary language.

A.W. HARRISON & SONS.
Electrotypers,
ENGRAVERS,
315 S. SHARP ST., — BALTIMORE, MD.

▶ In his book, Happy Days, Henry Mencken describes the Union Square he knew as a child,..."it was still almost rural, for there were plenty of vacant lots near by, and the open country began a few blocks away."[8]

The property had belonged to John Donnell, an early mayor of Baltimore. In 1847, his heirs gave a portion of it to the city to be used as a park. Then the family sold or rented the lots adjacent to the park for housing. This was a new method of private real estate speculation. The park enhanced the value of the properties. Union Square was the result.

▶ During World War II, the metal in the original fountain was melted down and sold as scrap iron to munition factories. It has since been restored by Mencken fans and you will note there is a medallion marker for each of his books embedded in the concrete.

3 Beside you is the Hollins Market. It was built in 1865 on land donated by George Dunbar. It is the last of the original market buildings in the city. Note its form: a low first floor for market stalls, and a high ceilinged hall above, which served, in the past, as a community center for social meetings, theater activities, club get togethers, etc.

Many of the stalls inside are owned by descendants of original marketeers. Why not stop in and chat with some of them? They love to reminisce.

Hollins Market.

T. Chandlee

4 Now we'll continue west on Hollins Street to Union Square. Pause and notice the building on the southwest corner of Hollins Street at Calhoun. It is one of the first branches of the Enoch Pratt library, opened in 1886. See the wonderful terra cotta and stone detail and the multicolored scalloped shingles. The building is a victim of the times and we wait to see its future.

▶ *Henry Mencken lived here from the year he was three until the year he died—except for the brief time during which he was married. He began to write in 1899 and his talents grew with such alacrity that during the 1920s he was considered to be the greatest literary force of the century. He was an editorial writer and columnist for the Sunpapers. He was also editor of the "Smart Set" and the "American Mercury", both of which were national magazines emanating from New York. He was known as the sage of Hollins Street. He shared both house and friends with his brother, August, who outlived him, and who willed the house with its belongings to the University of Maryland. In 1983, the house was traded to the city in exchange for the Pine Street Police Station. A friend has said that "H. L. Mencken, whichever Valhalla he is ensconced in, would be edified and greatly amused at the swap."*

T. Chandlee

Fountain in Union Square.

5 The corner of Hollins Street at Stricker is the southeast corner of Union Square, known to some because 1524 Hollins Street was the home of Henry Mencken. The Mencken family moved here from 813 Lexington Street in 1883. Henry was three years old. There was a large cluster of German merchants in this area and the Mencken family belonged to it. Mencken Sr. manufactured cigars. Their home has been restored and is furnished in many ways as it was when they lived in it. It is a museum and can be visited:

Wednesday-Sunday 10-5. Admission fee.

R. Jackson/Pratt Library

Henry L. Mencken.

6 Notice the fountain in the square. It was created to serve two purposes: one aesthetic and one practical. It made the park more attractive and it supplied water to the houses.

"Squares" became a popular form of housing for prestigious living in the 1800's as cities grew larger and people became richer. Generally they were constructed on hilltops where the air was thought to be more wholesome. Squares were away from the center of town but near enough to be an easy ride by horse and carriage. In the late 1830's the American and the Sun newspapers both complained because Baltimore was far behind New York in the development of such elitist neighborhoods.

▶ *Young Russell Baker lived near here in an apartment above a funeral home. He knew these houses well.*

> *...Lemmon Street was the black's street in our neighborhood. There they were tolerated as long as they didn't make an unsightly show of themselves around on Pratt and Lombard where whites presided....Until the night when Joe Louis licked Max Schmeling...I watched them march out of the alley and turn the corner...joined by other groups pouring out of other neighborhood alleys...into Lombard Street as though it was their street, too....Joe Louis had given them the courage to assert their right to use a public thoroughfare, and there wasn't a white person down there to dispute it. It was the first civil rights demonstration I ever saw and it lasted maybe five minutes.[9]*

▶ *In 1876 Bartlett-Hayward began to build huge round tanks known as "gas holders." During World War I it manufactured shrapnel shells. After the war the company developed a self-aligning coupling mechanism for ships. It was a versatile company which depended upon the immediate neighborhood for employees.*

THE JOHN H. JONES DISTRIBUTING AGENCY

238 S. MOUNT ST., BALTIMORE, MD.

HOUSE TO HOUSE DISTRIBUTORS OF ADVERTISING MATTER

Circulars, Folders, Booklets, Blotters, Cards, Papers, Almanacs, Calendars, Samples, etc. Distributed From House to House in an HONEST and INTELLIGENT MANNER by Competent Men. Signs Tacked and Parcels Delivered City or County :: ::

THE EXCLUSIVE DISTRIBUTORS ASSOCIATION

SINCERITY JONES SERVICE EXEMPLARY and ACME OF FIDELITY and JUDICIOUSNESS
C. & P. Phone, Gilmor 753-M

EMBLEMATICAL OF SAFETY TO ALL ADVERTISERS
Our Services GUARANTEED
We Give Personal Attention

We Want Your Work. We have been DISTRIBUTORS since 1899. We have BUILT A REPUTATION for an HONEST SQUARE DEAL towards all ADVERTISERS. We are ASSOCIATED with THE EXCLUSIVE DISTRIBUTORS ASSOCIATION. And You run no RISK when you PATRONIZE its MEMBERS, for each MEMBER carries a Price upon his OBLIGATIONS to you to Live Up To His CONTRACT, to Give You The SERVICE required of him, and in case of any losses he must make GOOD to the ADVERTISER or go Out Entirely. And the ASSOCIATION pays the Cost. You See It SAFEGUARDS You, and GUARDS the INTEREST and WELFARE of every LOYAL BROTHER MEMBER. So If You have never Tried Us, Give Us a Chance, to Show You That Our METHODS of REACHING The PEOPLE STANDS Out FAR-EXCELLENT. We Cover BALTIMORE, ANNAPOLIS and 42 County Towns. Our Price Is According to Bulkiness, Weight, and to Kind of SERVICE Wanted. Some ADVERTISERS want us to take Philadelphia and Washington, etc., But We Find Our Own Towns are All We want to Attend to, to do JUSTICE to The Work.
Address All Correspondence to

Walk around the circumference of the Square. It has become a popular place to live again and many of the houses have been recently restored by the young couples who currently live in them.

On the north side of the Square is the Steuart Hill School where a federal mansion named Willowbrook, built in 1799, once stood. A beautiful Adamesque oval room was removed from this house and is preserved in its entirety at the Baltimore Museum of Art.

7 Lemmon Street. This is an alley street and is where the laundresses, the cooks, the gardeners, the maids, who served in the large houses on Union Square had their homes. Real estate costs are more modest than some other downtown sections and most of the homes are occupied.

8 We'll walk back down Hollins Street to Carey Street. North on Carey Street is another one of our detours. South on Carey street takes you back to Pratt Street.

9 Turn east on Pratt to just below Parkin Street. This section is one of Baltimore's recent homesteading sections called Barre Circle. It is unique in that it has architectural unity. It was built by and for artisans only—hence there are no marble steps. The name is a new one—chosen by the city. The land was originally part of the estate known as Ridgley's Delight. Real estate costs are more modest than some other downtown sections and most of the homes are occupied.

10 Now we'll walk back to the B&O Roundhouse where we began. But as we go let's pause at Scott Street and have a moment's silence in honor of the Bartlett Hayward Company whose foundry occupied the block from 1837 until it was destroyed by arson in the 1980s. It was the home of Baltimore's cast iron fronts, the purchaser of the Winans Locomotive Works, the manufacturer of many elaborate pieces of cast iron furniture and architectural detailing. It was an important revered portion of the Baltimore scene for more than 100 years.

▶ Imagine the beauty of this small park when these homes were new. It was the epitome of out-of-the-city elegance. The idea of trees and space and wide walkways was just beginning to catch on in Baltimore. Only the well-to-do could afford it.

▶ In 1979 the Terrace was rehabilitated with federal monies. It is now cooperative apartments.

▶ The various religious denominations built expensive churches in the new squares in order to accommodate their wealthier congregations.

Walk north on Carey Street to Franklin Square. This was built between 1845-1875 and was one of the city's first suburbs. An omnibus had been established in 1844 and a horse drawn trolley in 1859. Thus, the city transportation system begun. People could travel from here into the city in a very brief time.

A Waverly Terrace is the name of the interesting group of Italianate houses which form the eastern border of the square. It was built in 1850 from a design based upon the English basement plan.[10] The cast iron balconies came from Bartlett-Hayward.

During World War II, west Baltimore became the home for defense workers who came from other states and who did not care about maintaining the appearance of the places which they rented. So lovely spots, such as Waverly Terrace, fell into major disrepair.

B Canby Row is the name of the group of brownstones which face the square on the south. Plans for the restoration of these houses are in progress.

C ½ block north at 217 N. Carey Street is St. Luke's Episcopal Church, built in 1853. The members of its vestry now live on the other side of town although the current rector has been successful in recruiting interest locally. It is a Gothic style church and it has some exquisite blue stained glass windows. Entrance may be gained by calling 523-6272.

▶ This was one of the first pieces of park land to be acquired by the city. It had been rented by the Carroll family to a German social group named the West Baltimore Schuetzen Association and Mount Clare was its clubhouse. In 1890, the city Park Board bought the house and 20 acres of land for $45,000. For a while the house was the home of the superintendent of Carroll Park. In 1917, the National Society of Colonial Dames of America in the State of Maryland assumed responsibility for the maintenance of the mansion as a historic house museum.

In its beginning, Mount Clare was much closer to the Patapsco than it is today because the water was higher. There was a story which described an underground passage from the house to the water which was to be used by Baltimoreans when Indians invaded their city. In 1970, the Colonial Dames invited Mr. Ivor Noel Hume from the Archeology division of Colonial Williamsburg to investigate this tunnel. The brickwork in the entrance was removed and Mr. Hume found an underground hollow area into which chamber pots had been emptied. The curiosity of the Dames had been aroused and it was this episode which precipitated the major digs.

The archeology has had several forms of adventure.

1. Soil analysis to determine what it had contained 200 years ago.

2. Cataloguing of numerous artifacts.

3. Ground sounding and digging for the foundations of a variety of dependencies or out-buildings.

4. Planning for the eventual restoration of the present acreage to its original status. The current hyphens are not the originals. Many would like to see them replaced. The bowling green in front of the house will become usable. And maybe, one day, the racing stable about which the barrister bragged will be found.

FOOTNOTES

8. Olson, *Baltimore: The Building*, p. 155.
9. Dorsey and Dilts, *Baltimore Architecture*, p. 81.
10. Stockett, *Baltimore History*, p. 102.
11. Ibid., p. 105.
12. Dorsey and Dilts, *Baltimore Architecture*, p. 86.
13. Stockett, *Baltimore History*, p. 142.
14. Beirne, *Amiable Baltimoreans*, p. 203.
15. Stockett, *Baltimore History*, p. 146.

Tour 4: The Shot Tower Neighborhood

1. Dorsey and Dilts, *Baltimore Architecture*, p. 107.
2. Stockett, *Baltimore History*, p. 158.
3. Ibid., p. 159.
4. Olson, *Baltimore: The Building*, p. 232.
5. Ibid., p. 229.
6. Dorsey and Dilts, *Baltimore Architecture*, p. 82.
7. Olson, *Baltimore: The Building*, p. 76.
8. Beirne, *Amiable Baltimoreans*, p. 377.
9. Stockett, *Baltimore History*, p. 159.
10. Dorsey and Dilts, *Baltimore Architecture*, p. 85.

Tour 5: Fells Point, the Original Port

Descriptions of the survey of Fells Point begun in 1967 in order to save the area from destruction are in the records of the Society for the Preservation of Federal Hill and Fells Point.

Tour 6: The Hopkins Medical Heritage

1. St. Patrick's Church, *"The Sequicentennial, 1792-1942"* (Baltimore: St. Mary's Industrial School, 1942).
2. William N. Batchelor, *"Recollections,"* (Baltimore: Church Home and Hospital, 1982).
3. Ethel Johns and Blanche Pfefferkorn, *Johns Hopkins Hospital School of Nursing* (Baltimore: Johns Hopkins University Press, 1954), p. 13.
4. Olson, *Baltimore: The Building*, p. 237.
5. Johns and Pfefferkorn, Hopkins *School of Nursing*, p. 83-4.
6. Julia B. Morgan, *"Women at the Johns Hopkins University: A History,"* (Baltimore: Johns Hopkins University Press, 1986) p. 1.
7. Morris Goldseker Foundation of Maryland, *"Annual Report,"* (Baltimore, 1981).

Tour 7: Butchers Hill & Patterson Park

1. Olson, *Baltimore: The Building*, p. 82.
2. William F. Cassidy, "Butchers Hill Restoring Urban Grandeur," *Real Estate News,* (March 1987), p. 15.
3. Beirne, *Amiable Baltimoreans*, p. 145.
4. Dorsey and Dilts, *Baltimore Architecture*, p. 122.

Tour 8: Federal Hill & South Baltimore

1. Olson, *Baltimore: The Building*, p. 138.
2. Ibid., p. 138.

FOOTNOTES

3. Mary Ellen Hayward, "Urban Vernacular Architecture in Nineteenth Century Baltimore," *Winterthur Portfolio,* (Spring 1981), p. 50.

4. Olson, *Baltimore: The Building,* p. 125.

5. Hayward, "Vernacular Architecture in Baltimore," p. 37.

6. Ibid., p. 38.

7. Ibid., p. 40.

8. Ibid., p. 40.

9. Ibid., p. 49.

10. Ibid., p. 57.

11. Ibid., p. 37.

Tour 9: Locust Point & Fort McHenry

1. Olson, *Baltimore: The Building,* p. 286.

2. Ibid., p. 306-7.

3. Ibid., p. 271.

4. Ibid., p. 384.

5. Beirne, *Amiable Baltimoreans,* p. 69.

6. Stockett, *Baltimore History,* p. 318.

7. Ibid., p. 320.

Tour 10: Otterbein Homesteading

1. Olson, *Baltimore: The Building,* p. 34.

2. Ibid., p. 34.

3. Ibid., p. 68.

4. Ibid., p. 186-7.

Tour 11: Early Southwest Baltimore

1. Dorsey and Dilts, *Baltimore Architecture,* p. 98.

2. Ibid., p. 96.

3. Robert L. Alexander, *The Architecture of Maximilian Godefroy* (Baltimore: The Johns Hopkins University Press, 1974), p. 86-92.

4. Stockett, *Baltimore History,* p. 130.

5. Ibid., p. 132.

6. Dorsey and Dilts, *Baltimore Architecture,* p. 152.

Tour 12: Mount Clare & the Railroad

1. Olson, *Baltimore: The Building,* p. 71.

2. Ibid., p. 72.

3. Ibid., p. 72.

4. Ibid., p. 73.

5. Beirne, *Amiable Baltimoreans,* p. 62.

6. Olson, *Baltimore: The Building,* p. 105.

7. Ibid., p. 124.

8. Henry L. Mencken, *Happy Days* (New York: Alfred A. Knopf, Inc. 1940).

9. Russell Baker, *Growing Up* (New York: Congdon and Weed, 1982), p. 205-6.

10. Dorsey and Dilts, *Baltimore Architecture,* p. 157.

CREDITS

Picture credits:

The Enoch Pratt Free Library
The Peale Museum, Baltimore
The Maryland Historical Society
The Flag House Museum
The Babe Ruth Museum
The Baltimore Sun
The Archives of the B&O Roundhouse Museum
The Johns Hopkins Medical Institutions: The Alan Mason
    Chesney Medical Archives.
Theodore M. Chandlee, Jr.

Cover Illustrations:

Painting: "Locust Point Marine Terminus in the early eighties"
    by H.D. Stitt, 1927. Courtesy of the B&O Roundhouse
    Museum.
Baltimore City Seal, 1963. Courtesy of the Baltimore City
    Archives — Department of Legislative Reference.

ABOUT THE AUTHOR

Priscilla L. Miles is a native of Baltimore, a graduate of The Roland Park Country School, The Union Memorial Hospital Training School for Nurses, the Johns Hopkins University, and the University of Maryland, Graduate School. She was a founder and first chairperson for the Baltimore Council of Historic Sites, Inc. She conceived and initiated Historic Baltimore Day. She is author of *Roland Park: Four Walking Tours And An Informal History.*

ACKNOWLEDGEMENTS

I cannot believe that a book can be written in isolation. This one evolved from an idea given to me by Sandra Hillman when she was the director of the Office of Promotion and Tourism. It developed with some walks and some talks with John Dorsey. My nephew, Timothy L. Bishop, architect historian, was doing some research on buildings which were to be placed on the National Historic Register. He shared some interesting facts with me and that cinched the writing of this book.

Caroline and Henry Naylor walked many blocks with me. Priscilla Long Beirne read everything to correct sentence structure, grammar and spelling mistakes. Catherine Miles Baxter read the manuscript looking for those words or phrases which were "just dead wrong." Jacques Kelly looked at it and corrected dates and historical facts. Theodore M. Chandlee helped with the selection of pictures and added some of his own.

Wesley Wilson and his staff in the Maryland Room of the Enoch Pratt Library were wonderful. So was Averil Kadis, publicity director at the Library. I made some new friends: Dorrie Young and Micheal Peach, in Otterbein, Evelyn Craig in Locust Point, Barry Richardson at the Indian Center, Rose Lamm and Grace Flack in Little Italy, and Geneva Taylor on Sharp Street.

My thanks to all of you.

FOR THIS BOOK

Editor: *Winnie Perilla*
Art Director/Cover Design: *Sandra R. Sparks*
Production/Page Layout: *Helen M. Carpenter*
Production/Maps: *Tim Miles, MCS Group*
Typesetting: *Brown Composition, Inc.*
Printing: *Quickee Offset, Inc.*